Women of Owu

Women of Owu

(An African Re-reading of Euripides' *The Trojan Women* first
commissioned by the Chipping Norton Theatre, UK)

Femi Osofisan

University Press PLC
IBADAN ABA ABUJA AJEGUNLE AKURE BENIN IKEJA ILORIN JOS
KADUNA KANO MAKURDI ONITSHA OWERRI WARRI ZARIA

ISBN 978 069 026 3
ISBN-13: 978-978-069-026-7

Printed by Lightning Source

Published by University Press PLC
Three Crowns Building, Jericho, P.M.B. 5095, Ibadan, Nigeria
Fax: 02-2412056 E-mail: unipress@skannet.com
Website: www.universitypressplc.com

WOMEN OF OWU

Some Reviews on its Tour of England (Feb-March 2004)

'...a rhythmic mix of chorus, song and dance punctuated by individual stories of woe... a thought-provoking piece.' – *Exeter Express and Echo.*

'...mesmerising... this play will stay with you with its thought-provoking themes.' – *Salisbury Journal.*

'Osofisan's version gives revitalizing vigour and voice to (the play's) ancient strength.' – *Edinburgh Guide.*

'...playwright Osofisan and director Chuck Mike have achieved something remarkable here—they have produced an extremely entertaining piece of theatre without in any way belittling their subject matter.' – *Oxford Times.*

'This African retelling (of Euripides), written by Femi Osofisan, of a people and a beloved city destroyed by the brutality of war is unnervingly topical and eloquently moving... A powerful evening of theatre.' – *Western Morning News.*

'In the ever-bourgeoning world of African playwrights and authors, arguably the most notable in recent times has been Nigeria's Femi Osofisan. His works have received numerous accolades and his international reputation places him at the pinnacle of the written and performing arts. However what is surprising is that he has managed to remain humble, and down to earth, remaining in touch with the struggles of his people and at the same time drawing inspiration from them.' –*The Trumpet.*

In this superb interpretation, leading Nigerian playwright Femi Osofisan has uprooted the play from its early Greek origins and slapped it firmly in Nigeria. The clear message is that this could be anywhere in the world where there's a war... Well worth seeing.' – *Bolton Evening News*.

A Note on the Play's Genesis

In 1821 or thereabouts, the combined forces of the armies of Ijebu and Ife, two Yoruba kingdoms in the south of what is now known as Nigeria, along with mercenaries recruited from Oyo refugees fleeing downwards from the Nigerian savannah land, sacked the city of Owu after a seven-year siege.

Owu was a model city-state, one of the most prosperous and best organized of those times. The Allied Forces had attacked it with the pretext of liberating the flourishing market of Apomu from Owu's control. Owu closed the gates of its formidable city walls, but it soon had to face the problem of drought when the rains stopped in the third year of the siege. This was a boon to the Allied Forces of course, and finally, in the seventh year they entered the city, and it was all over.

These Allied Forces, determined that the city must never rise again, reduced the place to complete rubble, and set fire to it. They slaughtered all the males, adult and children, and carried away the females into slavery. Owu was never rebuilt.

So it was quite logical therefore that, as I pondered over this adaptation of Euripides' play, in the season of the Iraqi War, the memories that were awakened in me should be those of the tragic Owu War...

F.O.

A Brief Production History

The first public reading of the play was given in 2003 by the Collective Artists in Lagos, under the direction of Chuck Mike. Some months later, in 2004,Mike again directed it for Collective Artists and the Chipping Norton Theatre, and the production went on tour of some theatres in England. With Tamara Malcolm as Executive Producer, Patricia Davenport as CSM and Akin Olatunji as Choreographer, it had the following Cast: Tunde Euba (Anlugbua, Gesinde), Tosan Edremoda Ugbeye (Erelu), Shola Benjamin, Louisa Eyo (Chorus Leaders), Medina Ajikawo (Orisaye), Louisa Eyo (Lawumi), Hazel Holder (Adumaadan), Rex Obano (Okunade), Funmi Olowe (Iyunloye), Amie Buhari (Young Woman of the Chorus),Ayo Thomas, Amie Buhari and Aliu Olafunji (Percussionists).

The version published here is a more recent version, and was given its first public production by the Okinba Players in a dramatised reading at the Arts Theatre in January 2005 with the playwright directing. It had the following Cast, in order of appearance: Mariane Ikems, Ronke Bamgbose (1st and 2nd Women), Emmanuel Fagbure/Gideon Tanimonure (Anlugbua), Tilewa Adeyinka (Erelu), Iyabo Amihere (Chorus Leader), Blessing Umeh (Lawumi), Osa Ogunmu (Gesinde), Ifeoma Ugwu/Deola Jimoh (Orisaye), Laura Uchegbu (Adumaadan), Oladele Akinseye (Mayé Okunade), and Tolulope Sanyaolu (Iyunloye). The Chorus Women were played by Emma Etta-Omini, Awele Aluka, Uju Okonkwo, Patricia Onuoha, and Tolulope Adenekan; while the soldiers were played by Odia Thomas and the other male actors. In the Production Crew were Alphonsus Orisaremi (Sets and Lights), assisted by Boyle Adikiba and Muyiwa Oluwole; Grace Hassan (Costumes and Make-Up), assisted by Yetunde Sokanla; Biola Olusunde (Music), assisted by Jaman Apina; Kachi Onwujiobi (Business Management); and Ben Iwuala (SM), assisted by Lola Adenugba. Iwuala was also Assistant to the Director.

Characters

ANLUGBUA: Former Owu war leader, son of Oba Asunkungbade, ancestral founder of Owu Ipole, now deified as *orisa*.

LAWUMI: Mother of Oba Asunkungbade, now also deified

ERELU AFIN: Wife of Oba Akinjobi, the reigning Olowu of Owu Ipole

GESINDE: Ijebu soldier, herald and staff officer of the Allied Army

ORISAYE: Half-mad daughter of Erelu, votary of the god Obatala

ADUMAADAN: Widow of Lisabi, first son of Erelu

ADEROGUN: Son of Adumaadan, grandson of Erelu

OKUNADE: The MAYÉ, Ife war leader, General of the Allied Forces

IYUNLOYE: Erring wife of the Mayé

CHORUS LEADER
CHORUS OF OWU WOMEN
SOLDIERS

SITUATION: *It is the day after the sack of the town of Owu Ipole by the Allied Forces of Ijebu, Oyo, and Ife.*

The night before, the king, Oba Akinjobi, had fled from the town, with some of his high chiefs and soldiers, leaving his family behind. The Allied Forces slaughtered all the men left in the town, including the male children; and only the female children and women have been spared, and made captives.

The scene is an open space close to the city's main gate, which used to serve as a market but has now been demolished. Visible in the background is the city itself, in ruins, and smouldering. Along the broken wall are the temporary tents of the old market, built of wooden and bamboo stakes, and straw roofs, in which the women are being kept.

The chorus of women, still invisible in the dark, is singing the dirge, Àtùpà gbépo nlẹ fẹlẹpọ*.

The god ANLUGBUA appears as an Old Man to two of the women sent to fetch water.

SCENE ONE

ANLUGBUA: Tell me, dear women—
You seem to come from there—
What's the name of the city I see
Smouldering over there?

WOMAN: Stranger, you don't know? Look at
My tears! That was once
The proud city of Owu, reduced to ruin
Yesterday—

---

* This song, and all the others that will be mentioned later in the text, will be found in the Appendix at the end of the play text, together with their approximate translations in English.

1

ANLUGBUA: Ah! Just as I feared!

WOMAN: Those soldiers you see revelling
In the camp over there *(Points)*
Dancing and drinking to their victory—
And may Anlugbua choke them with it!—
They were the ones who came yesterday
And scattered our lives into potshards....

ANLUGBUA: Yesterday!

WOMAN: Yesterday, old man!
For seven years we had held them off,
These invaders from Ijebu and Ife, together
With mercenaries from Oyo fleeing south from the
Fulani forces. They said our Oba
Was a despot, that they came to free us
From his cruel yoke!
So for seven years they camped
Outside our walls, but were unable to enter
Until yesterday, when a terrible fire engulfed the city
And forced us to open our gates. That was how
They finally gained entry and swooped on us...

ANLUGBUA: I don't understand:
You said all this happened only yesterday?

WOMAN: Yes, and I'd advise you to hurry away
As fast as you can, Old Man, for if they catch you
Your life won't be worth a beetle. They are
Not sparing the life of any male that falls
Into their hands, whether old or young.
Yesterday on the orders of their leader,

2

Okunade, the Mayé,
And before our very eyes here,
They rounded up all our husbands and
Brothers, and sons, and slau—
(Stops, choked by emotion.)

WOMAN: They slaughtered them! All!

ANLUGBUA: All?

WOMAN: Not one was spared! Not a single male left now
In Owu, except those who escaped the night before
With our king, Oba Akinjobi.

WOMAN: And—shame, oh shame! Our women were seized
And shared out to the blood-splattered troops
To spend the night. Only some of us—we two, and
The women you see over there
Were spared, those of us from the noble houses
And others whose beauty struck their eye:
We are being reserved, they say, for the Generals.

ANLUGBUA: But your priests! Your chiefs! Your diviners!
Why didn't anybody call me?

WOMAN: Call you?

ANLUGBUA: My words were clear enough, I thought!
Whenever any grave danger threatens the town,
I said! Whenever some misfortune arrives
Too huge for you to handle, run
To my hill and pull my chain!
How was it that no one remembered?

WOMAN: You... you... who are you?

3

ANLUGBUA: Three times, I said! Call my name
Three times, and I shall be back,
Sword in hand, to defend you!

WOMAN: Sword! That would have served little purpose
This time, I tell you! Because—eh! Yeh!... Yeh!
What did you say? You... you... *Mo gbe!*...
Is it you...? Have I stumbled upon...
Impossible! My eyes have not seen a...
No! Impossible!

ANLUGBUA: Calm yourself, my dear women.
You have nothing to fear!

WOMAN: It's not you, is it? Let me not
Go blind today! It's not you, *orisa* Anlugbua?
Not our ancestor they talk so much about?

ANLUGBUA: I said—

WOMAN: But—(*Screams*) So it's true, ehn?
Help! Help! The god is here!
Anlugbua is here! Come and see!

ANLUGBUA: (*Hard*):
Sh! Quiet, I said! Calm yourself,
I don't want to be announced! Not yet! You hear!

WOMEN: (*Cowed*)
Yes... yes...

ANLUGBUA: So go on, tell me all that happened here.

WOMEN: (*Whimpering with fright*)
Ah... ah...

ANLUGBUA: *(Softening).*
Listen, this city was very dear to me.
I was there when your grand parents built up
The little old village of my father into a fortress,
And called it Owu.
I, Anlugbua,
Great grandson of Oduduwa, progenitor of
The Yoruba race.
Together with my great uncles,
Obatala the god of creativity
Orunmila the god of wisdom
And Ogun the god of metallic ore,
We came down from our house in heaven
And lent our silent energies
To the labour of the workmen. Unseen, of course.
Then Esu bore our wishes up to Edumare,
The Almighty Father, and
Slowly the bricks and the stones and the clay
Grew into a city enclosed within two walls
And a moat around it like a girdle: Owu,
The safest place in the entire Yorubaland.
But now I return to see— the unimaginable!
A city reduced to rubble.
How did this happen?

WOMAN: Ancestral father, the armies of Ijebu, Oyo and Ife,
Who call themselves the Allied Forces,
Under the command of that demon
Mayé Okunade,
Caused this havoc.

ANLUGBUA: Okunade? Not the man I knew? Gbenagbena
Okunade, the one endowed by Obatala

5

With the gift of creativity, to shape wood
And stone into new forms? The fabled artist
Who also dreamed those arresting patterns on virgin cloth?

WOMAN: The very one! But when his favourite wife,
Iyunloye, was captured and brought here, and given as
Wife to one of our princes, Okunade became bitter, and
Swore to get her back. Shamed and disgraced,
He abandoned his tools and took to arms. And so fierce
Was his passion for killing, that he rose rapidly
Through the ranks, and soon became the Mayé!
An artist? He's a butcher now!

ANLUGBUA: How sad! How really sad!

WOMAN: That's the latest sign of his new calling now,
That ruin you are looking at, Anlugbua!
All your shrines drenched in the blood
Of your worshippers,
All your sacred symbols wiped out by fire!
Right up to the grove of your mother,
Lawumi, whom we have always venerated, Anlugbua,
Mayé and his men pursued their victims, and
Cut off their heads. Then they
Stuck them on stakes which they carried in triumphant
Dance off to their camp, over there.

ANLUGBUA: Even my mother's shrine!

WOMAN: All night long and all of today
The invaders have been looting our city,
Turning it into a wreck, violating
Our sacred shrines and groves. Now, they are
Back in their camp, each of these pirates

6

To sort out the plunder, and allot
Our city's riches to their soldiers and servants.

WOMAN: Meanwhile they make us wait here in abject terror,
Expecting the worst, and
Unable even to mourn our sons and husbands.

ANLUGBUA: No more: I understand:
It is the law of victory, the law
Of defeat.

WOMAN: Mayé besieged our city for seven full years,
Because of a woman, and would not go away!
For seven full years, the people of Owu
Suffered and refused to open the city gates.

WOMAN: Seven years without rain they were, seven years
Of failed harvests. All those terrible years
Where were you Anlugbua?

ANLUGBUA: You did not send for me! You know
The oath I made forbade me to return
Here, unless you sent for me!

WOMAN: After three years, the city
Began to starve of food and fruit,
And the streets stank of disease and death.
But we never ceased
To worship you, or pour libation at your shrine!
Where were you, Anlugbua?

ANLUGBUA: When I was leaving the world—when I dipped
My sword into the earth and became a mountain—
I left an iron chain for you, and I said,
Pull it whenever you need me—

WOMAN: How we needed you all the time!
            It was a war, such as we had never known before:
            The Allied Forces came with weapons they call guns
            Guns, Anlugbua! Deadly sticks
            Which explode, and turn a whole battalion
            Into corpses. Rags upon rags of bleeding flesh!

WOMAN: Among us
            Not one man had ever seen a weapon like that!
            But the Ijebu troops brought them in abundance!
            They got them, we learnt,
            From their trade with the white men on the coast!

WOMAN: Against these terrifying guns, Anlugbua,
            Your people had only their blades and incantations.
            Where were you?

ANLUGBUA: Well, it's all over now.
            The Allies have got what they wanted.
            I've come too late.

WOMAN: Too late to help us. But
            Not too late to witness our final rout.

WOMAN: Not too late
            To relish this massacre they call a war.

WOMAN: Nowadays,
            When the strong fight the weak, it's called
            A Liberation War
            To free the weak from oppression.

WOMAN: Nowadays, in the new world order, it is suicide to be weak.

ANLUGBUA: It's very sad, my dear women! But

8

Still, with all your tears, I, Anlugbua,
I am the real loser here.
Gods do not cry. But that only makes the pain deeper still.

WOMAN: So what do you want? What have you
Come back for? So that we may pity you,
We ourselves who ache for consolation?

ANLUGBUA: I ask you—without a shrine, without worshippers,
What is a god? Who now will venerate us?
Who sing our praises among these ruins?

WOMAN: Go back to your heaven, Anlugbua,
And learn also how to cope with pain.
If only you gods would show a little more concern
For your worshippers!

WOMAN: Goodbye, ancestor, we cannot help you.
We must return now to our own burden, and
Join the other women
To prepare for our life of slavery.
(They go).

ANLUGBUA: I confess, I am broken. Farewell, my lost city.
Farewell, my dear women, whose arguments
Shame me. But I promise
This will not be the final word in the dirge.
*(He goes. Dirge rises. Lights expand now, and pick up ERELU
AFIN, where she sprawls on the ground.)*

SCENE TWO

ERELU: Ah, am I the one sprawled on the ground like this,
In the dust, like a common mongrel! Me!
But what's the use getting up? To go where,
Or to achieve what purpose? Of course I am sorry for myself,
But so what? When fate has decided to strike you down
What amount of crying can help?
That's what I keep telling myself. I say—Resign yourself,
Erelu Afin, and accept it all with forbearance!
But Nature is weak: my tears pour out nevertheless!
(She cries, as she sits up).

CHORUS LEADER: Oh, we shed our own tears too, Erelu Afin!
Can one ever be strong enough against misfortune?
In spite of our courage, disaster drains us!

ERELU: Who will look at me now, and remember
I was once a queen here, in this broken city, .
Or that in that palace over there, now burning to ashes
I gave my husband five splendid sons?

WOMAN: We remember, Erelu, just as we also recollect,
That one by one, yesterday,
Before our very eyes, the invaders cut their throat,
All those handsome princes.

ALL: Yesterday. .

ERELU: And my daughters, dear women!
These same eyes saw my daughters
Seized by their hair, their clothes ripped off their bodies
By brutal men, and their innocence shredded forever
In an orgy of senseless rapine.

10

WOMAN: Erelu, we still hear their screams tearing through
The air, tearing our hearts.

ERELU: My daughters—remember, they were all
Engaged already to be married to kings! Already,
Remember, the palace was bustling with their bridal songs,
Chants of dancers and drummers
Rehearsing for the day—

WOMAN:, We remember the songs too well, Erelu,
And the dances:
We composed most of them!

ERELU: Now those laughing girls
Are going into the kitchens of uncultured louts!
And your songs—each word a blade of mockery now—
Sink quietly down our throat!
Ah, I am talking too much! Forgive me, I beg you,
It's because of my eyes: they have grown weary
With crying, and frozen against my wishes.
Talk is the only weapon I have left for mourning.

CHORUS LEADER: We know, Erelu. Go on talking. Be strong.

ERELU: Oh I wish I could die, die! Or fall silent
In a hole where sorrow can no longer reach me!
Who will save Erelu Afin? Who can save me now?

WOMAN: Yes, who will save us?
*(Erelu falls to the ground and the dirge, '**Lèsí ma
gbàwá ò**' rises. She joins in the singing for a while)*

ERELU: Oh you Ijebu beasts!
And the animals from Ife who are your allies!

11

You Oyo mercenaries who have been made homeless by
The Fulani, and so must make others homeless too!
All of you men over there preparing to return home
After destroying our city! My curse upon you!
May you never again know the soil of your motherlands!

WOMAN: *Tuah!* I spit and the wind dries it!
          May each of you be sucked and withered by the wind
          Of affliction on your journey back!

CHORUS LEADER: You that have turned our once-flourishing city
          Into a relic of history, may you all without exception
          Suffer the indignity of unremembered graves!

WOMAN: Liars! You came, you said,
          To help free our people from a wicked king. Now,
          After your liberation, here we are
          With our spirits broken and our faces swollen
          Waiting to be turned into whores and housemaids
          In your towns. I too, I curse you!

ERELU: Savages! You claim to be more civilized than us
          But did you have to carry out all this killing and carnage
          To show you are stronger than us? Did you
          Have to plunge all these women here into mourning
          Just to seize control over our famous Apomu market
          Known all over for its uncommon merchandise?

WOMAN: No, Erelu, what are you saying, or
          Are you forgetting?
          They do not want our market at all—

WOMAN: They are not interested in such petty things
          As profit—

WOMAN:	Only in lofty, lofty ideas, like freedom—
WOMAN:	Or human rights—
WOMAN:	Oh the Ijebus have always disdained merchandise—
WOMAN:	The Ifes are unmoved by the glitter of gold—
WOMAN:	The Oyos have no concern whatsoever for silk or ivory—
WOMAN:	All they care for, my dear women All they care for, all of them, is our freedom!
WOMAN:	Ah Anlugbua bless their kind hearts!
WOMAN:	Bless the kindness which has rescued us From tyranny in order to plunge us into slavery!
WOMAN:	Sing, my friends! Let us celebrate Our new-won freedom of chains! *(They resume their dirge, till Erelu's sudden wail of anguish cuts them off abruptly.)*
CHORUS LEADER:	Your cries of anguish, Erelu Afin, Are like the talons of a hawk clawing at our breasts They pierce our ears with terror. But we have been Defeated, what is it you advise us to do?
ERELU:	Look at the camp in the distance Where the soldiers are preparing to depart.
WOMAN:	Yes, we can see them, loading their horses—
WOMAN:	Pulling down their tents—
WOMAN:	Pulling out the smouldering logs, Extinguishing fires—

13

WOMAN: Tying up their bags—

WOMAN: Filling up the giant casks of water—

ERELU: They are preparing for their journey back home!

CHORUS LEADER: Yes, of course, they are leaving. What do you suggest we do?
             (Erelu wails again.)

WOMAN: What can we do?
             Soon, we know, all of us will be shared out
             Some to become concubines to the officers

WOMAN: Some to be domestic servants,

WOMAN: Some to be sold off
             To the slave caravans going north to the Arabs

WOMAN: Or south to the ships of the white men.
             (As Erelu wails, enter the two women we saw earlier.)

WOMAN: We have seen him! We have seen him!

CHORUS LEADER: Who?

WOMAN: We have seen the ancestor, Anlugbua!

WOMAN: What! *(Shouts of surprise, shock, disbelief, etc.)*

WOMAN: Just now, over there! It's true!

WOMAN: Both of us, we saw him! Spoke to him!

WOMEN: *Ope o, Anlugbua!* Salvation's arrived at last!

CHORUS LEADER: Come out there, you women of Owu Ipole,

All you who have lost your husbands and your innocence
Come out and—!

WOMAN: No, listen—

CHORUS LEADER: Cast off your despair, I say, and with a song of defiance
Dare to look at the burning wreck, and salute our fallen men!

WOMAN: No! No!

WOMEN: No what?

WOMAN: We saw him, but... it's not salvation yet!

WOMEN: No? What do you mean?

WOMAN: Anlugbua came, but
He has returned to heaven. We are on our own!

WOMEN: Liar! Impossible!

WOMAN: It's true!

WOMAN: *Yeah! Ye-pah!* He's gone?

WOMAN: He told us himself of his helplessness!

WOMEN: Then it's not him you saw!

WOMEN: He cannot abandon us like that, not him!
Not our ancestral father!

WOMAN: He has. He left in defeat. We are on our own.
(General wailing.)

CHORUS LEADER: No, stop the wailing and brace yourselves
My dear women. The lesson is clear. It's us, not the gods,
Who create war. It's us, we human beings, who can kill it.

15.

WOMAN: How? What can we do? What power of suasion
Do we have over these bloodthirsty men?

ERELU: Ah, raise your dirges again, without trembling, even if
For the last time, women! It's much better than
Our needless questions: Start the song:
For those who survive, there's always another day
(They begin the dirge; Lèsí gbọ́ gbìgbì léreko o?):

CHORUS LEADER: *(To others off-stage)*
You wretches in there, cowering in despair
Like all of us, come out I said, and
See for yourselves! While our conquerors
Prepare the first phase of our enslavement, our brave gods
Run to hide in their heaven! Come out now,
And join us, all of you!

ERELU: No, my dear woman, I beg you, not all.
At least let my poor Orisaye continue to remain inside,
Out of sight for now. These events, as you know,
Have made her even more delirious than she was,
And her state of incoherence would only worsen
To see her mother like this.

WOMAN: But what will they really do with us, Erelu? Please,
Say something! My imagination is killing me!

ERELU: In defeat, dear women, always expect the worst.
That is the law of combat. The law of defeat.
(To herself)
Look at me! A slave! To whom will they sell me?
To the flesh merchants of Kano or Abomey? Or
Straight to the white masters in the cold castles
Of Cape Coast? Will they put padlocks

16

On these wrinkled lips, and chains on these old and
Withered feet? Ah, they will brand me with their hot iron,
Me! I am going to be maid to some foreign matron:
I will watch night and day over her brats,
Or slog away in her kitchen, picking vegetables,
My body covered in sores! Me, the Erelu of Owu!

CHORUS LEADER: Erelu, worse trials are still ahead. Help us.
Preserve your strength so we too can preserve ours.

WOMAN: Worse trials than these? Is that possible?

WOMAN: It will be hell for me. I know, away from these familiar streets.

WOMAN: And me! Even if these hands can weave again, Anlugbua.
It will never be here in the joyous looms of Owu?

WOMAN: Ah, just think of having to clean their toilets!

WOMAN: Perhaps I will be lucky enough to be carried away
To the Ijebu kingdom. There, I'm told, life is always pleasant,
Even for slaves. And being close to Lagos makes jewels cheap.

CHORUS LEADER: What!

WOMAN: Anywhere at all
Will be better for slaves than the forest lands of Ife...

CHORUS LEADER: No, my friend, you don't understand! Nowhere
Will it ever be pleasant to be a slave! All we can
Is counter misfortune with our spirit, and our will.
So, let us dance my friends as we wait, as
Our mothers taught us to do at such moments.
Dance the Dance of the Days of Woe!
*(They resume the dirge and dance, slowly, as lights
fade out on the scene into a Blackout.)*

17

SCENE THREE

(Lights return. Scene as in Scene ONE. The god ANLUGBUA stand-ing, alone. In the distance, the women sing the dirge, 'Ìjì ayé pọ̀'. Enter LAWUMI.)

LAWUMI: Anlugbua!
         (Seeing her, he makes to leave.)

LAWUMI: No, don't go away, listen to me first.

ANLUGBUA: Yes?

LAWUMI: It's about Owu, your city.

ANLUGBUA: My former city, you mean?
           You're satisfied, I hope, with your work.

LAWUMI: So you know.

ANLUGBUA: It had to be you, mother! That such
           A disaster would happen here, and I not know
           About it. But why did you do it?

LAWUMI: They had to be punished!

ANLUGBUA: For what offence? What could they have done
           So unforgivable as to merit this?

LAWUMI: Arrogance, that was their sin! An insufferable display
         Of arrogance towards me, towards Ile Ife, where
         We all come from! Yes, it's true
         That your father founded Owu, but it was only
         With the help and blessings of Ife!
         It was because he, a priest, married a princess

181

Of Ife—me!—that my father agreed to give him a crown
And make Owu one of the seven kingdoms
Of Yorubaland. Is that a lie?

ANLUGBUA: No, but—

LAWUMI: Owu forgot its history, forgot its origins!
Your people became drunk with prosperity!
And in their giddiness, they dared to send their army
Against Ife! Imagine it!
They razed the town down and reduced it to dust!

ANLUGBUA: But are you forgetting, mother? It was
The Ifes who first attacked Owu, at
The market of Apomu—

LAWUMI: Because the Owus were selling
Other Yoruba into slavery! It was a law, wasn't it,
Laid down by your royal uncle and my son Sango
That no Yoruba should ever sell other Yoruba
Into slavery! But the Owus would not listen!
Flagrantly at Apomu, they broke the law, and
The only way to stop them was by force!

ANLUGBUA: This amount of force, mother? After all
Ife could have tried other means of persuasion. Besides,
Common sense advises that you don't send out your soldiers
Against an army far superior to yours!

LAWUMI: Good, let the Owus eat that superiority now!
They sacked the Ife army, and took back
The Apomu market. But that was their undoing,
Because I led them on. I made them attack

19

The Ijebu traders at the market too.
Yes, I made sure of that! Recklessly
They looted the stalls of the Ijebu, killed many
And sold the others into slavery! And of course
As I expected, the Ijebu rose in response
And sent their dreaded army up against the city.
That was the beginning of the story
Whose consequences you see now before you!

ANLUGBUA: Well, I hope you are satisfied now!

LAWUMI: No. The city is in ruins, all right, but I'm not satisfied.

ANLUGBUA: No? What more can you want, mother?

LAWUMI: These Allied Forces, they need to be punished in their turn.

ANLUGBUA: What!

LAWUMI: I say I want to punish these invaders who have
Just plundered your town! Will you help me?

ANLUGBUA: So that's why you finally decided to bring me into it!

LAWUMI: I need your powers.

ANLUGBUA: But it doesn't make sense, mother! These soldiers
Are your allies. It was you egged them on,
As you just confessed, for seven years!
Seven punishing years that took their toll!
You stopped them from breaking camp
When boredom and fatigue, disease and death
Would have sent them back to their homes. And now,
Now they have helped you win your long-sought victory,
You say you want to punish them?

20

LAWUMI: Because they too, they have no regard for me.
Just imagine, when they set the town on fire,
Desperate men and women ran
To my shrine for protection. But do you know,
These Allied Forces, the very soldiers
I gave my total support, did not spare them!
Can you believe the insult! Yes,
Of course the fugitives were Owu people and so
Were enemies, but so what! They had run to me
For refuge! Me, their ancestral mother!
But no, the Allied soldiers did not care for that!
They seized them all! Even Princess Orisaye,
Obatala's vestal votary, was
Literally dragged out of my hands, without
Any of the soldiers protesting! Then,
To cap the insult, look! They have set fire to my shrine!

ANLUGBUA: To all our shrines, dear mother!

LAWUMI: And will you then let them get away with such sacrilege?
You will not help me punish them?

ANLUGBUA: You know, in that, I'll be only too glad to oblige you.
But tell me first, what's on your mind?

LAWUMI: I want their return journey to be filled
With grief: Human beings, it is clear, learn
Only from suffering and pain.
Already Esu has promised me, there'll be
Such confusion at every crossroads
They'll never find their way.
The hunters' god, Orisa Oko,
Will turn the forests against them, such that

21

For many, the home they will be returning to
Will be the stomach of beasts.
You, my son, can make
Their journey even more agonizing
By unleashing your terrible storms
On them. Send your shafts of lightning
Wherever they gather, and pound them
With awesome thunderbolts.
Let everyone of them perish
Till human beings everywhere learn
That the gods are not their plaything.

ANLUGBUA: And Ogun, the god of war, who is the protector
Of these soldiers, what does he say?

LAWUMI: Even he, my son, even Ogun is angry!
His shrine was one of the first to be desecrated!

ANLUGBUA: Then, it shall be done as you wish.
LAWUMI: That's all I want. Come with me.

(They go. The dirge rises as the lights return us to the women.)

SCENE FOUR

(Enter GESINDE. He goes to ERELU AFIN)

GESINDE: Erelu Afin, I'm sure you remember me,
Gesinde, herald to the Allied Army, and special aide
To the Mayé, General Okunade. I am the Ijebu officer
Who has been coming back and forth these seven years
Through your gates, bearing messages from our generals.

ERELU: Yes, I remember you, Gesinde. As I remember how
Your appearance always meant some doom to our people.
Go on, talk. What further misfortune
Do you have for us this time?

GESINDE: Your majesty, I wish you'd understand,
I am only a messenger, just a borrowed mouth. It's the Generals
Who take the decisions. And now they send me to tell you to prepare:
Each of you is going to your future masters.

CHORUS LEADER: Separately or together?

GESINDE: What a question! Separately of course.

ERELU: Without exception? No special consideration
At all for any of us?

GESINDE: Such are my instructions.

ERELU: Not even for me? Nor for my sick daughter Orisaye?

GESINDE: Oh she's fortunate. Balogun Kusa himself has asked for her.

ERELU: To be a servant to his wife? Now you
Confirm my worst fears.

23

GESINDE: You're wrong there Erelu. He does not want her
As a servant. She is going to join his harem.

ERELU: You mean, he will marry her?

GESINDE: That's his intention, as far as I know.
And that should make you erase your fears.

ERELU: But... Orisaye's the bride of a god! He should know!

GESINDE: He does.

ERELU: She's been wedded since birth to Obatala, our god of purity
And creativity. And the god insists that she remain a virgin—

GESINDE: That's exactly what excites the Balogun about her, the fact that
She is still a virgin. His eyes dance just to hear her name.

ERELU: And how does he think Obatala will—?

GESINDE: The Balogun is a protégé of Ogun, don't forget.
He knows Ogun will not let him down.

ERELU: So because of his lust, he will pitch one god against the other!
Ah my daughter, what will men not dare just to satisfy
Their greed! It's over now, Orisaye, all your life of piety and
Devotion! It's all been a waste...!

GESINDE: But Erelu, I don't understand you! You are unhappy, that your
Daughter is going to share the bed of a king?

ERELU: Forget it, you'll never understand. You are a servant
Used to taking orders. But what of my second daughter,
Beautiful Adeoti? What have your generals decided for her?

GESINDE: She is, er... fortunate too. We have er... sent her to a safer place.

24

ERELU: Where? Is she still alive, still able to respond
To the tremor of the drums?

GESINDE: She has gone where pain can no longer reach her.

ERELU: Where, tell me? What is that look in your eyes?

GESINDE: *(Silence)*
Please don't insist, Erelu. I'm only a servant, as you say.

ERELU: *(Sighs).* And my other daughter Kesobo, the Shy One?

GESINDE: Wife of your fallen hero Sàkúlà? He was a good soldier, and
Fought gallantly to the end. The Generals admire that.
That's why his widow will go to Otunba Lekki, whose legend
I am sure you are all familiar with by now.

WOMAN: What, herald, of Iyunloye? What will happen to her?

GESINDE: Where's she?

WOMAN: In there, with the rest.

GESINDE: Let her wait there, till the Generals decide.

WOMAN: With all this destruction she's caused, I hope that—

GESINDE: Quiet! I say the Generals will decide! But I assure you
Her wronged husband will soon be coming, and if like me
You've seen him in battle, you would not want to be
In her wrapper when he arrives! Now, let me—

ERELU: I am not the widow of a hero. Only an old woman
With fallen breasts. Without this stick to lean on,
I could not stand alone by myself. Age, you see,
My son, has turned my limbs to banana stalks

25

And rendered them useless for any task:
What will happen to me?

GESINDE: Balogun Derin has asked that you be allocated to him.

ERELU: What, that dog! That double-dealing liar! Ah, Anlugbua!
Please, Gesinde, anybody else but him!

GESINDE: You know I cannot help you.

ERELU: Weep for me then, you women of Owu! Now
I know what it means to suffer defeat.

CHORUS: And what about us? You've not spoken about us,
Officer. What's to happen to us?

GESINDE: What else do you think will happen to riff-raff?
Your case is simple enough. But it won't be your turn,
Till we've finished sorting out the big fish. So just wait here
And continue to behave yourselves.
(To GUARD)
You, go in there and bring out Princess Orisaye,
She's to join Balogun Kusa's camp immediately.
And—what's that? A fire in there?
Join him inside, all of you!
Quick! Stop any of the women there trying to be heroic
By burning herself. We Ijebus are civilized, and
Have our code of conduct: we will not allow bush people
To embarrass us with any barbaric act of self-destruction.
Put out the fire!

ERELU: Ah poor you! So you can be so easily frightened by a little fire!
What you think is a human body set ablaze is just my daughter
Orisaye, running around with a torch. The war has affected her
Badly and she's... well, no longer in control of her senses.

26

GESINDE: Bring her out here. Put out the torch!
(*ORISAYE runs out, with a burning torch*)

ORISAYE: No! Leave me alone! Get your own light,
Don't steal my own!
I am going to be married to a king, don't you know?
This torch is for our bridal night! See, how the flame dances
Prettily, gracefully
To the waves of our passion! Ah,
All the gods are awake with us! Their watchful eyes
Follow us with blessings
As I go to the bed of my king!
(*Sings 'E súre fún mi' and dances*)

ERELU: Orisaye, my daughter—

ORISAYE: Mother, you're crying! Is it because
Of my brothers fallen in battle?
Wipe your tears, that is an old tale now.
Today we are celebrating, for
I am going to be given away in marriage to a
Warrior king! What a promise of luxury!
Mother, you should be laughing and singing for me!
The air should be ringing with your prayers!
Or is it that you cannot see very well
In this surrounding darkness? Take this then,
I brought it for you!
(*Holds out the torch.*)
Won't you take it? You think it will burn you?
No, don't be afraid, I lit it myself when I heard the news.
Some words are such that when we hear them, all the light
Inside us dies at once, and our smiling daylight
Turns into the bleakness of night. I lit the torch

27

So I will not have to grope my way to the camp
Where I shall be married to my enemy, that handsome butcher
Of our people.
Mother, pray for me! Pray that this torch may burn
Brighter and brighter, so I do not miss my footsteps
On the way to my husband's bed! He calls, listen!
He calls! What are we waiting for?
Dance with me, my friends, to the call of my beloved!
Raise your voices, sing with me!
(Begins to dance and sing 'Ọlọbẹ̀ ló lọkọ o?' *till she grows delirious.)*

CHORUS LEADER:Hold her! Hold her, Erelu, she will burn herself!
She's out of her senses!

ERELU: Come, my daughter, give me that! Let me hold it for you.

CHORUS   She's out of her senses. Insanity is the drug of misery.

ORISAYE: What? You think I'm mad? *(Laughs)*
They think I am insane, mother! But it is not madness,
It is something called fear! Yes, I am afraid!
I fear that, at the crucial moment, my courage will fail me,
And I shall not be able to proceed to Kusa's tent.
So promise me, mother! Promise
That if you see me stumble, you will rush at once to my side
And help me on! Promise
To push me into the Balogun's arms
And have him carry me off on his splendid horse! Then
In his bed, where we shall consummate our marriage.
I shall take my revenge!
Yes, I swear it to you, mother, this wedding will be
Kusa's dreadful, unbreakable pact with death!

My presence shall bring such suffering and anguish
To his household, to his city and his people
That the wreck they have caused here will seem in the end
Like a joyous feast. I will destroy them
Totally, totally, without remorse! They will rue the day
They set out to conquer the city of Owu!
So, women, rejoice! This is no time at all for crying!
Let us rather dance and celebrate! Happiness is coming!
All our dead will be avenged!

ERELU: Not by you, my child!
You will be a slave, even in the palace of Kusa,
Under constant watch.
You will be completely helpless—

ORISAYE: Only till I put a blade to his lovely throat...

ERELU: Ah! *Ọmọ mi,* Orisaye*!*

ORISAYE: And I'll watch his blood flow, gurgling like fresh wine
From the palm tree! I will be singing, mother!
Then of course they will seize me, and hack me to death!
Ah, what happiness is waiting for me!

ERELU: My child—

ORISAYE: As for the others, you will see.
They will never make it back home, will never again see
Their wives or children! They will not—

CHORUS LEADER: Please Princess, that's enough. You're embarrassing us
With these futile prophecies. Making your poor mother
Shake before these barbarians. Enough now.

ORISAYE: All right, I will keep quiet. They have heard enough anyway
To know what's coming to them. I will say no more.
But wipe your tears, mother, and all of you.
Victory for our conquerors will be a very brief affair.
Orunmila has revealed it all to me. *(Laughs).*
Only a few will ever make it back home, and when
They do, they will find, waiting for them there, not peace
But new rulers, strange conquerors
Who in their absence would have taken over
Their land and their wives!
(To GESINDE)
This will be the harvest of your escapade here.
A defeat worse than our own.
At least our men died on our soil here,
Where gentle hands could close their eyes
And cuddle them home to our ancestors. But you!
You are cursed already to end on the road of battle and plunder.
How I pity you!
So my dear women, suspend your dirges! Let us sing and
Dance instead for the victory that is coming!

WOMAN: How sweet your words, Princess! If only
I could believe them! But it's no use: one look alone at you
And at ourselves is enough to jolt us back from fantasy.
Give up! All your ranting and prancing cannot save us
From the pain we know is coming!

GESINDE: I'm glad to see that one of you at least still has her senses.
But for the fact that this one has lost hers,
She would have learnt very quickly how dangerous some words
Could be in a careless mouth!
(Cowed, the women sing, 'Lèsí gbọ́ gbìgbì léreko o?'
Gesinde steps aside).

30

This is another evidence of how the people we revere
And hold in high esteem are sometimes noble only from
A distance. When you get close to them
They are just as foolish and witless as the commonest folk!
Who could have imagined for instance that a warrior
As redoubtable as Balogun Kusa,
A man feared from Nupe to Dahomi, would allow himself
To be smitten by a mad woman? Of all the fine women available
Here, some even dying to lick his foot! But no, it's
A hare-brained woman, a lunatic whom a poor fellow like me
Would never have looked at twice that Balogun desires!
Great men are sick! Perhaps that is why they are up there
And we down below.
But, young woman, that's enough,
We've got to be going.
All those words, as they told you just now, cannot change a thing.
So just follow me without any further trouble.
As for you, Erelu, wait for me here.
I'll be coming back for you as soon as Balogun Derin
Gives the word. His wife, I assure you, is a pleasant woman
And being her servant won't be as bad as you fear.

ORISAYE: May a thousand termites eat your mouth for that word,
You insolent Ijebu dog! Servant!
Is it my mother your dare address like that!
You murkier than the murkiest maggot in the market
Of leftovers! You junk, listen to me! I say listen to me!
You are wasting your time, you hear? My mother is not going
Anywhere with you! She is going to die here on the soil of Owu!

GESINDE: Not if I can help it, young woman!
Suicides may be heroic, but that will only ruin my career!

31

ORISAYE: You're pathetic, soldier! Who's talking of suicide?
That'll be too convenient for your generals.

GESINDE: How's she going to die then? Who'll kill her—one of these women?

ORISAYE: Wouldn't you like to know!

GESINDE: I warn you, women, that—

ORISAYE: Save your breath, I am not going to tell you, although
Everything is here on my palm, including your future, swine!
Tell Balogun Derin, the gods have decided his fate
His home is only three weeks of trekking away from here,
But tell him, it's going to take another seventeen years
You hear? Seventeen whole years before he reaches it!
And they'll be years of wandering and suffering and
Fighting without respite!
O women, rejoice, all these men have been marked down
For a fate much worse than yours, and
When they know, they will envy us our defeat!
So let's go, animal! Take me quickly to my husband
Who is waiting to die in my arms.
Let dirges accompany us to our wedding
Since Kusa is determined to taste the food
Reserved for a god! Together. we shall know
A most violent death. as
Obatala. up in fury, turns our wedding party
To a funeral feast!
So goodbye mother, I can't wait to join my husband
On our journey to perdition.
Goodbye. but not for long. because your end too
Is near, and we are going to meet again soon. Yes.
Both of us will be reunited when I lead down

A procession of corpses from the house of Kusa.
Sing! Sing my wedding song!
*(She begins the 'ẹkún ìyàwó', 'Jọwọ o dúró, sisí', which
the Chorus pick up as she dances out.*
ERELU AFIN faints.)

CHORUS LEADER:Hold her! Erelu has fainted! Hold her!
Help her up!
(They help her up.)

ERELU: Leave me, take your hands off me!
           Did I ask for your help? Why do you bother?
           I want the earth to open like a mouth and suck me in! There,
           At least, in the dark indifference of her womb
           I may be able to rest at last from pain.

WOMAN: Erelu, *iya wa*, your royal majesty,
           All is not finished yet: Let us pray to the gods—

ERELU: The gods! Which gods!
           Do you still trust any of them after this?
           Or have you so quickly forgotten what they told us
           About Anlugbua just now?
           (Points to the burning city)
           No, women, there is no shelter anywhere
           But in ourselves! Each of us has become our own god.

WOMAN: Does that mean we are all alone now, abandoned?

ERELU: We have always been alone, my dear women. Only
           We did not know it.

WOMAN: There's no hope at all then, of escape?

ERELU: None. Think of when you were last happy.
           That may strengthen you.

33

WOMEN: What? That will only worsen our pain! Or was it not only yesterday
That we were dancing and celebrating on the streets, when
We woke to find the invaders gone from our gates?
(The Women speak now in Alternating voices)

WOMAN: We looked across the walls, and the enemy camps were
Deserted. No smoke or movement, no horses in sight—

WOMAN: Ah, *Idupe o, thank you Anlugbua*! Relief at last!

WOMAN: They had grown weary at last, the invaders!
That was what we thought...

WOMAN: After seven years of fruitless siege, of trying without success
To enter our city, and with so many of their men dead
In the attempt, we thought they'd given up
And gone back to their homes—

WOMAN: A shout of joy went up, swept through the streets
In the mouths of gongs and fevered drumbeats!

WOMAN: It grew into a roaring torrent, sweeping into every house!

WOMAN: Kabiyesi was dancing! Our Oba was dancing!

WOMAN: He and the war commanders!

WOMAN: A celebration! They ordered a celebration!

WOMAN: Our travail was over —

WOMAN: The starving ended—

WOMAN: The work of weeding and planting could start again— ·

WOMAN: The season of weddings could resume—

34

WOMAN: The wounded could now begin to heal! —

WOMAN: Oh, such was the happiness in the air —

WOMAN: Only yesterday!

WOMAN: And then,
While we were dancing and laughing, the first birds
Came flying across the wall—

WOMAN: Heralds of horror and death,
They came with flaming brands in their talons—

WOMAN: Hawks in their hundreds, carrying torches—

WOMAN: Hundreds upon hundreds, bearing flames,
A hideous armada of fire —

WOMAN: And they began to alight on our thatch roofs
Setting them alight! —

WOMAN: In the blink of an eye, the whole city, ablaze!

WOMAN: Our homes, our compounds—

WOMAN: Fire, everywhere!

WOMAN: Our silos, our garrisons—

WOMAN: Huge balls of smoke! Screams in the air!

WOMAN: Fire, fire, everywhere!

WOMAN: Smoke everywhere! It was hard to breathe!

WOMAN: The gates! The gates! Open the gates!

35

WOMAN: We rushed, all of us,
In a mass towards the gates, the only escape now
From the flames—

WOMAN: Yes, in our panic, we hacked the gates down,
Spilled out of the burning city—

WOMAN: And ran out blindly into... *Horror*!

WOMAN: They were waiting for us, our enemies!

WOMAN: *Yee-pah!*, they had not gone away!

WOMAN: *Yee-pah!*, they were still there—

WOMAN: Waiting for us with their guns!

WOMAN: *Yeeah*! They had only retreated into the forest,
To hide, to deceive us!

WOMAN: And now they were rushing back, rushing
Towards us, with fire in their guns!

WOMAN: Shooting, killing, mowing down our men!

WOMAN: Our sons! Our daughters!

WOMAN: Our sisters! Our mothers!

WOMAN: Our friends! Our leaders!

WOMAN: Horror! Horror, everywhere!

*(Softly they begin the dirge 'Welẹ Welẹ leri nsẹ o', as they return
to their places.)*

WOMAN: And that was it, Erelu! You know yourself:
           That was the story of yesterday
           And of our last moments of happiness

WOMAN: That was how our city went down,
           The city in which we were all rejoicing
           With our husbands and our children
           Only yesterday—
           (The dirge rises for a while.)

ERELU: You are right. Happiness is a fake.
           The gods employ it as a mask to trick us each time
           They are about to plunge us into grief.

CHORUS LEADER: But we never remember that, we human beings.
           We are always eager to forget that the sky is at its calmest
           In the moments before a mighty thunderstorm.

WOMAN: That was why we rushed headlong into celebration,
           And came crashing down on the waiting rocks of disaster.

WOMEN: Farewell, beloved city. Farewell to happiness.

ERELU: All the same, I beg you,
           Let us not be too harsh on ourselves. We are
           Only human beings after all. Against the pettiness
           Of gods and goddesses, we have no defence.
           Our priests, remember, told us our tribulations are the work
           Of our ancestral mother, Lawumi. Let us be consoled then:
           This defeat is her shame.

CHORUS LEADER: I agree with you, Erelu. And instead of cringing,
           Let us raise our voices and curse these men!

37

WOMAN: Yes, you over there, listen, we curse all of you!

WOMAN: As we curse all men!

CHORUS LEADER:Sing! Sing! In defiance of their whips!

WOMEN: We curse you all!

CHORUS LEADER:Of their insults!

WOMEN: We curse you all!

CHORUS LEADER:Of their rapine and assault!

WOMEN: We curse you all!

CHORUS LEADER:Our curse on all men, and especially men of violence!

WOMEN: We curse you all!

CHORUS LEADER:All those born of women, but who use us as dogs!

WOMEN: We curse! We curse!

(They start a ritual song of malediction, ? 'Ọrun dẹẹdẹ dẹ bi orin arò' and, as it grows into a frenzy which climaxes in their baring their breasts collectively, they shout: 'WE CURSE YOU ALL!!!' Immediate BLACKOUT.)

SCENE FIVE

(The following day. Same place. The Women's dirge, 'Wẹlẹ-wẹlẹ leri nsẹ o' wakes us to the rising dawn.)

WOMEN: Dawn has broken again, and we are still here.
Two days now without a wash; two days of waiting,
Stinking in our underwear. We have stayed like this,
In these make-shift tents, watching our city burn to ashes.
Two days they have prolonged our fears, as we wait
To be assigned to our different masters. Our conquerors,
The Ijebu and Ife generals, have been arguing, we hear,
With their Oyo mercenaries over the sharing of the loot.
For the two days we have been praying to our gods, in vain.
They are no longer listening to us.

CHORUS LEADER: Look, Erelu: someone's coming.
(ERELU does not look.)

WOMAN: It's Adumaadan, widow of your slain son, Lisabi.
She is bringing a baby strapped to her back.
(ADUMAADAN arrives.)

WOMAN: It's her son, Aderogun. Your grandson, Erelu.

CHORUS LEADER: Where are you going with your son?

ADUMAADAN: Where else but to my new master? They allowed me
To come and fetch whatever I can from the rubble.

ERELU: Ah poor woman! That I should live to see a day like this!

ADUMAADAN: What's the matter, old woman? Who has been bitten, and who
Is now bleeding and moaning on her behalf?

39

ERELU: Everything that happens to you touches me too, you know.

ADUMAADAN: Since when? Dear mother-in-law, you had only one son
Whom you loved, as far as I remember. It was not my husband.

ERELU: If Dejumo himself were alive now, I'm sure, he would tell you
It's not true. I loved him and his brother equally
Just the same way I mourn their death.

ADUMAADAN: Well, his brother's death does not move me.
Right from birth that man brought the curse of death with him
From heaven. But, against the priest's instructions, you refused
To have him destroyed. Now it is he who has destroyed
Us all, exactly as predicted. Because of you,
Because of your pride which you disguised as a mother's love,
Now I am a widow about to be mated with the very man
Who murdered my husband!

ERELU: All of us are losers, now, we women of Owu. You lost a husband,
Me a king, five brave sons, and a daughter—

ADUMAADAN: A daughter? What of your other daughter then?

ERELU: Adeoti? What about her?

ADUMAADAN: So you've not been told?

ERELU: What?

ADUMAADAN: Poor woman, you've never liked me, and I on my side
Have not liked you either. But I cannot but be sorry for you now.
Your other daughter, Adeoti, is dead.
I found her body lying at the entrance to the shrine of
The goddess Lawunmi. Her throat had been cut.
(General shout of lamentation, ending in the dirge,
'Bùjé-bùjé pa mí o'.)

40

ERELU: Oh! Oh! Is that what that goat Gesinde
Was trying to tell me yesterday and I chose to misunderstand?

ADUMAADAN: I closed her eyes and poured some sand on her.
In the situation, it was all I could.

ERELU: Thank you! Ah, Deoti, you too!
Slaughtered like a goat and abandoned to the flies
Like offal! And such a beautiful woman! What a waste!
Goodbye to you, my dear daughter. *Orun re o!*
(As she chants Adeoti's oriki, the Chorus dirge softly
in the background: 'Ara mi, ę woro tíkú fi ṣe wá'.)
My daughter, I give you the same words of lament
That I had hoped you would say one day
Over my grave. Sleep well with our ancestors...
Adumaadan, wife to my slaughtered son,
Thank you again. I wish I knew
What deity to pray to now to reward you
For the kindness you showed to my daughter. All the gods
We knew seem to have turned their back on us!
So all I can say is, please accept
These hands of gratitude from a broken mother's heart.
(She offers her hands, joined-together into an 'osu' of respect, to
Adumaadan.)

ADUMAADAN: You know you don't have to thank me. I loved the Princess,
And I also cry for her. But if you ask me, it's myself I pity now.
Deoti is dead at least, she can no longer feel any pain.
How much luckier then than the rest of us who are still alive,
Who have been spared perhaps only for greater torment!

ERELU: Don't speak like that, my child. Death
Is sweet, we think. But it is easier to talk of it,

41

Than to welcome it. We do not know
What is on the other side, whether it is better or worse
Than here. Whereas even at its most bitter,
Life offers hope at least, which death does not.

ADUMAADAN: Hope? What hope has a dog tethered to the belt of Ogun?
I was happy once, glad to devote myself totally
To the care of my husband and to raising his children. I won
A reputation for that, and see, it's what has ruined me now.
They say it's because of my devotion and fidelity
That my husband's killer specifically asks for me
To be given to him! And that's what frightens me even more,
I confess. For I am only a woman, with a woman's familia'
Weaknesses. Our flesh too often, and in spite of itself,
Quickens to a man's touch,
And a night of loving is all it takes, they say, to tame
The most unwilling among us. I am scared
Therefore that this animal in my body will betray me,
That against my wishes, against my memories,
It will begin to respond eagerly
To the new man even as it once did to my husband!
How can I think of that and call it hope?

CHORUS LEADER: You are lucky, princess, if that is all the suffering you fear.
Even in misfortune, which levels everyone, the portions are unequal:
We dare not tell you what we believe will be coming to us.

ERELU: My daughter, you won't like to hear this
But my advice is—do like the reed in the bush. Stand and strut
In good weather. But when it storms, learn also to bend.
Your husband is dead, you have a son to raise, the only
One left now of his father's lineage. Therefore for his sake,
And for the survival of this glorious family about to fade
Into the mists of oblivion, dry your tears;

42

Surrender your pride, and learn to
Give to your new man the care you once gave my son.

ADUMAADAN: Are those words from you! You! Old woman
Did I not say you never loved my husband!

ERELU: That boy's his only son, I repeat. If he lives, we do not die.
And one day therefore, he will grow up and remember,
And we will be fully avenged.

ADUMAADAN: No! I will not listen to—
(Enter GESINDE)

ERELU: What do you want again this time, man of misfortune?

GESINDE: The boy. *(Turns to ADUMAADAN)*. Please don't hate me.

ADUMAADAN: You want to take my son?

GESINDE: It's the order of the generals.

ADUMAADAN: What will you do with him?

GESINDE: I would rather not say. Please don't insist.

ADUMAADAN: Then I won't part with him.

GESINDE: Please, *ayaba*, it's my orders.

ADUMAADAN: You're going to kill him?

GESINDE: Well...

ADUMAADAN: Tell the truth, you slave and stop dithering! Out with it!

GESINDE: It was Balogun Derin, *ayaba*. He warned his colleagues
Very strongly that their future would not be safe after this,

43

If they went away from here, and left a single heir
To the Owu throne alive. So it's no use resisting.
Give him to me.
(As she resists).
It's more dignified, believe me, not to resist.
When you have lost a war, you have lost, and there's nothing
You can do about it but to accept the consequences. The law
Is what we say it is now, and has to be obeyed.
Right now, my instructions are to take this child away and—

ADUMAADAN: And kill him?

GESINDE:. Of course! Why are we wasting time? You'd do as much
To us if your side won the war. Now hand him over,
It's hard enough what I have to do.

ADUMAADAN: I can't… please…

GESINDE: Perhaps I should let you know—in case some of you
Are nursing some stupid hopes in that direction—your king—
Your husband, Erelu—we caught him in the night, and
He has already paid the price of his folly. You
Must have heard someone screaming for a long time, begging
For death. That was him, in the hands of the Generals.
But luckily it's over now for the poor man. So, *ayaba*,
Don't imagine anyone can help you now. Give up the child.

ADUMAADAN: You've got my father already, as you say. Why not spare—

GESINDE: Take it from her!
(The soldiers advance towards her.)

ADUMAADAN: No! Don't you dare touch me, you dogs!
Move back!

44

Get away from me!
(She straightens up, bravely, unstraps the child and gives him to GESINDE.)
Right, here you are,
Have him. Go and do with him
As you have been ordered.
(As GESINDE turns to go.)
No, wait! Let me hold him a little
Just once more. Please.
(GESINDE gives the child back to her, and turns aside. As he speaks, the women raise the dirge, 'Şe mba mọ...' in the background.)

GESINDE: It is hard, this life of a soldier, when one
Has to witness a scene like this. And it is going to be
Harder still, I know, when we bash
The child's head against a tree,
And crush his skull as we've been ordered to do.
They say it's taboo to shoot him
Or cut his skin with a blade.
Yes, the generals sit back and give their orders,
But it's we poor ones who have to face the victims
And spill the blood.
(To ADUMAADAN)
I know how you feel, *ayaba*. But I am a soldier
And I must do my duty. Try and be brave.
(She hands the child to him. He and the soldiers leave. ERELU AFIN collapses, as the women resume their dirge.)

CHORUS LEADER: *Pagidariiii!* Raise the dirge, my dear companions.
There goes the last hope of our land! Cry the people of Owu!

Your last lamp is about to be extinguished! The gods
Have done their worst to wipe us out:
But they too will die without worshippers!
(The dirge rises, fills the stage,
The MAYÉ, Generàl OKUNADE enters, with a detail
of armed soldiers.)

MAYÉ   All right, enough of that! *(The singing stops)*.
Good, I don't want to hear even a single sigh of sorrow,
This is a happy day!
Yes at last, such a glorious morning!
It's here,
At last, the day I've been waiting for, dreaming about!
The woman is in my hands at last, that
Shameful whore I called my wife! There she waits now,
Inside there, trussed up with others
Like a common slave! Yes, Iyunlóye!
Who would believe it? They say
It was because of her that I abandoned my first vocation,
Left my work as an artist, and took to arms.
Perhaps.
But in truth, it was more because of Prince Adejumo,
The dog who stole her from me. Now
He is gone, felled by one of our ordinary soldiers.
And it is her turn.
I am going to make her suffer as much as she made me.
She'll beg, and crawl in the sand till both her knees
Are in tatters. And then I'll kill her.
What I've not decided yet is
Where—whether here, among the very ashes
Of the city where she came to enjoy the fruits
Of her licentiousness,

46

Or to take her back home with me
And release her into the arms of the numerous women
Turned into widows by this war, and
Let them lynch her! Yes!
Or—even better still—
Give her to the children grieving inconsolably
Over the loss of their fathers.
You and you—go inside there and bring her here.
No, drag her out by her hair! I want to hear her screaming
For mercy as she comes, her nose dripping with snot!

ERELU: Oh you gods, how strange your ways!
So you are still there after all, giving pain one moment
And then joy the next! So with all your mischief, you can still
Mete out punishment to whom it is due!
I salute you, Mayé, for being the hand of justice!

MAYÉ Do I know you?

ERELU: Kill your wife, Mayé Okunade, and you will have my blessings.

MAYÉ What strange prayers! What's she done to you?

ERELU: I am the Erelu Afin of Owu. That should tell you who I am.
It was my son your wife bewitched and led us to this calamity.

MAYÉ Ah, so it's you! Misfortune has undone you too,
! see. But that's the logic of defeat. What did you say?

ERELU: Have Iyunloye put to death, as you swore just now!
Let her death be slow and cruel. But be careful!
When they bring her out here, turn away your eyes, I beg you,
Don't look at her.

47

MAYÉ   That's a funny request.

ERELU: Mayé, I know what I am saying! Women like her are dangerous,
            Especially to their lovers. Once they catch you, you're hooked
            For ever: They have such powers of enchantment, eyes
            That will set cities ablaze. You know what I am talking about,
            The proof is over there. One look at her again,
            Believe me, and all your anger will melt away

MAYÉ: Rubbish. But I don't blame you, you have no idea
            How badly she hurt me, or how much I feel betrayed—

ERELU: But that's it, Mayé! Anger and desire are twin sisters
            In this drama we call love, two kernels in the same nut!
            Especially where the passion has been deep
            Like yours, love can too easily rekindle. Take my advice,
            Mayé, don't look at her—
            *(The soldiers drag IYUNLOYE out, roughly, with her of-
            fering no resistance. She is conspicuously beautiful, even
            in her rough state, and has obviously taken some care to
            spruce herself up a bit. As she appears, some of the
            women gather around her quickly, singing a song of
            abuse, 'Ɔkɔ-ɖɔkɔ o!'.)*

IYUNLOYE: Get away from me! Leave me alone!
            My husband, you see how they treat me!
            (He turns his eyes away.)
            Listen, whatever may have happened, I am still
            Your wife at least, and everybody knows it.
            So this contempt is also a slap on your face!.

MAYÉ: *(To the women).* Leave her.

ERELU: Too late! Now you have looked at her!

48

MAYÉ: *(To the soldiers).* Move back.

IYUNLOYE: *(Looking at him.)*
You look good, I must say, in your fighting attire.

MAYÉ: Thank you, but this is no occasion for that.

IYUNLOYE: I used to wonder about it a lot. You, whom I only knew
As an artist, now a commander of battalions!
I just could not picture it in my mind.

MAYÉ: And now you've seen with your eyes. It never occurred
To you, did it, that it was your perfidy drove me to it?

IYUNLOYE: You should be grateful to me then. See, from a
Common artist, you've become a man of power. The Mayé!
And it certainly fits you too, to look at you!

ERELU: Mayé, remember what you came to do! Don't let her—

IYUNLOYE: Do you miss it—I mean, your former life? It's what
Has helped me survive, I can tell you. I mean, during these years
Of our separation! It's what I had learnt
All those years I was following you from market to market,
Selling your *adire* cloth that I remembered:
The way you drew the patterns, waxed the cloth with care,
And then dipped it into the pot of dye.
That's what I've used here to build up a thriving market
And establish myself as a woman to be reckoned with.
Without your nurturing, my dear husband, I would not be here!
That's why my most famous design, known all over
From Kano to Porto Novo to Kumasi is called '*Faari*
Okunade'—named after you. But you must know all that already—

MAYÉ: Traitor! So you have no repentance at all? No shame?

IYUNLOYE: Not about you, or what you mean to me, you who raised me
To be a woman, and was the first lover I ever knew.
Even if you hate me now it won't change the truth: Of all
The men who have used this poor body for their pleasure,
You alone, you are the only man I've ever loved.

MAYÉ: I did not come here to argue with you. You've always
Known how to handle words.

ERELU: Mayé, don't—

IYUNLOYE: Tell me, my husband—and don't mind the old woman,
Because you are the only one I can ask the question—
What punishment has your army decided for me? Am I to die?

MAYÉ: You have been sentenced to whatever fate I decide.

IYUNLOYE: Then I am glad! I—

MAYÉ: I have already decided. You are going to die.

IYUNLOYE: My husband!

MAYÉ: Stop that!

IYUNLOYE: So be it then. I know from the past how pointless
It is, trying to plead against your decisions. So I accept.
What I cannot accept however is your bitterness.
Seven years now I've missed you, longed for you, cried for you!
And now at last, I find you again, there's a big wall of anger
Between us, between your tender hands and my trembling lips!
Please, my husband, I know I have wronged you,
But, even if only as a last favour to someone you once cherished,

50

Give me a chance to explain. I beg you, my dearest husband,
Don't let me go with only your curses to accompany me.

MAYÉ: No!

IYUNLOYE: Anybody can kill. But it is not everybody who can forgive, or
Who can be just, as I know you are.
That is why I am begging you to listen to me. Please!
(The women sing their song of abuse again.)

ERELU: Let her talk, since she wants to, Mayé. She thinks she is clever
But when she has finished I will be here to answer back.

MAYÉ: *(After a pause)*
All right then, go on, but be brief.

IYUNLOYE: Since you are looking for blame, why not start
With this woman here? She it was after all who mothered the man
Who captured me. Ask her, and she herself will confess that
At his birth, the priests ordered his immediate
Execution. They warned that he was evil,
That if he was left to grow up, he would bring disaster
To Owu. They said he would seduce a woman, and through
That act cause the death of many. But she chose instead
To hide him and nurse him to manhood.
So who but her's to blame? It may be the weakness of a loving
Mother, but I am the victim of it: I have been the helpless
Tool of fate, used in spite of myself to fulfil a prophecy.

MAYÉ: Fine story! But from the reports that came to me
You went willingly enough!

IYUNLOYE: When the Owu forces attacked us at the market
At Apomu, you were not around, remember?

You had gone back to Ife then to bring more supplies.
There was no one I could call upon for help! ·
You must have heard what the soldiers did to us,
You are now a soldier yourself!
They sacked our stalls, looted our wares,
Killed the men and—what they did to the women!
In desperation, I had to buy my life with the only asset
I had—my beauty! It's the truth, my husband!
Akogun Awalona led the assault, ask him!
He brought me to Owu, and gave me
To the king's youngest son.

MAYÉ: You joined his harem, and forgot about me. Perhaps
       Because I was only an artist—

IYUNLOYE: But how or in what way has that ever diminished you?
       You were an artist when I met you and married you
       And I've always been proud of your work!

MAYÉ: An artist has only his dreams. He has no power.
       In the palace, on the other hand, sunk
       In opulence and pleasure, it was easy for you to lose
       Your head, and forget.

IYUNLOYE: Never! I never forgot you, I swear! But
       There was no news about you for months.
       Your designs were no longer on sale anywhere.
       At Apomu, nobody remembered you. How was I to know
       That you had merely changed profession
       And joined the army? Everyone said you were dead, that
       On your way back from Ife, you were caught in a crossfire.
       I was in despair, and captivity made it worse.
       To mourn you, I decided to use my position in the palace

To revive your art. And now,
Through the numerous markets controlled by Owu agents,
I have made your adire cloth famous
All over the world. The most popular pattern of them all
Bears your name. What more proof do you require
To know I've never stopped loving you? Listen,
This is how we advertise it:
(She tries to begin the song, dancing seductively, but is cut off by Mayé.)

MAYÉ: Enough! For seven years now
We've been outside here at your walls. All that time
You were missing me, pining for me,
You didn't hear, even once,
That I was present here with the troops—?

IYUNLOYE: Of course I heard. And how many times I tried to run away
To join you! On a number of nights I climbed up the walls,
Tied ropes together, and tried to escape. But the guards found me out
Each time and stopped me. It's the truth! I had to bribe them
To keep it to themselves. Ask them, they are my witnesses!
I really tried, my husband! Look in my eyes!
See if I am lying to you!

CHORUS LEADER: Don't look in her eyes, General! All you will find there
Are danger and deceit!

WOMAN: Speak up quickly Erelu, for all of us! Don't let her
Get away with it! Her honey tongue is about to betray us all!

ERELU: I will answer her, have no fear. Perfidious woman,
Why do you mock the dead like this?
So you tried to climb over our walls to escape!

53

And the guards caught you several times and stopped you!
How admirable, how terribly courageous of you!
It just happens that all those guards you summon
As your witnesses are dead, slaughtered by our conquerors!
Have you forgotten then that I myself came to you,
On many occasions during the siege, appealing to you
To leave the city and return to your husband?

IYUNLOYE: It's a lie!

MAYÉ: Don't interrupt! You had your say!

ERELU: Many times I offered to lead you through one of our secret exits,
So you could go and intercede for us with your husband's
Forces. If you'd gone, the war would have ended years ago,
And certainly without this catastrophe we see now.
But did you listen to me? All you did was play me along,
Agreeing to go when it seemed we were about to lose
The war, and then quickly changing your mind
When fortune turned on our side! So what's this story
About loving or missing your husband? Listen,
It's time to face the truth and stop lying!

IYUNLOYE: You're the liar, old woman! You—

ERELU: Confess, you liked my son, and
You liked his city! Dejumo was handsome, young,
Strong and wealthy. It was a breath-taking sight watching him
Ride a horse! And he had in his stable some of the most
Magnificent breeds. I know as a woman how it feels
To be chosen as the favourite of such a man. Besides,
Who would rather live in backward Ile-Ife than the city
Of Owu, if given the choice? When you gave yourself up

54

In Apomu, and were brought here to Owu, you saw suddenly
Such wonder as you had never imagined! You saw
Our city walls and our paved streets! Crowds that made you
Dizzy; the silk on the women, coral beads on our neck,
Gold in our hair! You were dazzled! Confess!
And then the jewels my son used to spoil you with! Soon
The small and wretched hamlet of Ife became a distant
Dot in your mind. That's why you stayed my dear.
That's why you couldn't go back to your husband. And
In the end, you also stole his talent to enrich yourself.

IYUNLOYE: Yes, be cruel! Be arrogant! Boast of your riches,
Of your dazzling streets! So Ife is backward! Go on,
Jeer at us because we are a minority people!
My husband, you see the kinds of insult I've had to swallow
These many years here! The dirt they poured daily
Down my ears! Ife is wretched, Ife is small, Ife is bush!
Just as we condemn the she-goat, before eating it.
But, old woman, the skin that graces the king's shoulders,
The leopard knows who supplied it. When
Mother Goat nods at the sonorous sound of the drum,
She is not dancing! It is because, each time it sounds,
She recognizes the wailing of the leather! Without
Our sweat and our labour in Ife, tell me, just where
Would Owu be? Without the profits from our markets
Which your warriors seize from our women;
Without the yams and fruits you plunder from our farms,
How would you feed? How would you be handsome
Without the jewels beaten out of our bronze factories?

ERELU: What are you saying? Don't divert the argument:
It is the fate of the conquered to toil for the strong!
That is the logic of war, the logic of defeat!

IYUNLOYE: But you and your chiefs always claimed, before this,
Didn't you, that we are one and the same people in all of
Yorubaland? So this is what you meant: the monkey
Does the work, while the baboon eats the food!

ERELU: That is not the point now, shameless woman! We are talking
About you, and how you made good for yourself.
Any other woman in your place would have shaved her hair,
Splashed herself in sand and ash, and flung herself
Down in the dust, grovelling at her husband's feet!
But not you, not the Queen of Lust herself! No!
Instead of that, you have come out decked
As if for a festive dance. Shame on you! Shame!
Mayé, you've heard her. She talks of rights, not of you,
Not of what she made you suffer. She doesn't talk of your men.
You'll be a fool to believe her. I've done my part. Remember,
You have a reputation to defend, and must punish her
Without mercy or remorse! Let her serve as an example
For all women like her who have no shame but would
Rather spend their life in depravity!

CHORUS LEADER: Mayé, it's as she says: you have a duty to your ancestors,
And to the memory of all the men who fell here,
To make her pay. Do not hesitate. History is waiting.

ERELU: It won't wait for long, I assure you all. Nothing she said
Has changed my mind. The penalty for her offence, as she herself
Knows, is death by stoning. It's a quick exit, shorter and kinder
Than the long penance we suffered here. Take her to the soldiers.
(She falls and clings to his knees.)

IYUNLOYE: My husband! Pity, my husband!
*(Begins to chant his oriki, but he cuts her off with a
gesture.)*

56

Please, any other punishment but that!
I know I hurt you, but it was not me, believe me.
Just my misfortune as a pawn in the hands of men! Beauty
Makes all women vulnerable to the greed of men, as
You know, and when the men are powerful, our will
Is nothing! Such men just ride over us as they wish. That was
My problem, believe me! As you once loved me, please
Forgive me now! Don't kill me! Give me another chance!

ERELU: Ask her what chance she gave them, those soldiers
           Who perished here. And I am not talking now only of the men
           Of Owu, but your own soldiers, Mayé—your friends,
           And the families they left behind.

MAYÉ: Enough, old woman, let me speak. *(To soldiers.)*
           Take her to my tent. Let her join my caravan.

CHORUS LEADER: Just now, General, you were going to have her stoned to death.

MAYÉ: That is what is going to happen to her all right. But at home,
           Not here. The punishment will be sweeter, when carried out
           By the women of Ife. Especially those who search, but
           Do not see their husbands return.

ERELU: In that case, let her not ride with you. Put her in another caravan.

MAYÉ: Why should I do that?

ERELU: For your own sake. When a man has loved a woman,
           The way you have done, that love never dies.
           At an unsuspecting moment it will spring awake again,
           Like a snake from sleep, and strike...

MAYÉ: That's because you don't know how deep it is, the wound
           She inflicted on me. That love I had for her can never

57

Wake again, I assure you. Still I'll take your advice.
We'll put her in some other caravan. When we get back
To Ife, she'll pay the full price for her life of infidelity
And waywardness, and serve as an example to others.
*(He goes, as IYUNLOYE is led off. ERELU, content, initiates a song of celebration: 'Òjò ayò kán sí mi lára ...'
Enter GESINDE, with soldiers carrying the body of
ADEROGUN.)*

CHORUS: Look, look! It's the body of your grandson, Aderogun, or
What remains of him—

CHORUS LEADER: Will the horror never end then? See, they've crushed his head
O Anlugbua, and now they bring the battered body to us!
O when will the horror end?

GESINDE: Erelu, the caravans are all leaving, except for the last one
Which is to carry you and the rest of the women.
Otunba Lekki has taken your daughter-in-law Adumaadan
With him. He had to leave in a hurry: news came that someone
Has seized his father's throne and started a war back home.

ERELU: So my Orisaye was right! From one battlefront to another!
War never ends, but only moves to another place?

GESINDE: I have a message for you from Adumaadan.
Poor woman, as they were leaving,
She broke off and ran to the mound where her husband Lisabi's
Body is buried, and knelt there, crying for a while. It was
Such a moving scene that it brought tears to my eyes. Then,
Turning to me, she implored me to ask you to bury her son
For her, this boy whose head we dashed against the araba tree.
In place of a shroud to wrap him in, she sends this war-dress

58

That his father used to wear. The sight of it, once,
Sent Lisabi's enemies scampering from the battle field
Until we arrived. Normally of course it should belong to the man
Who killed him. But the Otunba thinks, quite rightly,
That the sight of it hanging in his bedchamber among his other
War trophies might upset Adumaadan when
She comes into his house. He's such a sensitive man,
You see, even though he gave the orders to kill the child.
But it's the logic of war, the law of defeat. So, go on,
Give him the final rites. I've had him washed already,
As you will notice, in the stream on our way here.
That should make it fast, so we can leave at once. To make it
Faster still, I'll go and have a grave dug for him.
*(ERELU takes the child. GESINDE leaves. The dirge, 'Ara
mi, ẹ woro tíkú fi ṣe wá' rises.)*

ERELU: Ah, is this your body I hold in my hands,
You innocent child?
(She sings his oriki:)
Cowards! How can you be so frightened of a child?
Even when we were strong, and had all our bravest commanders
Around, you still conquered us and sacked our city.
Now they are all dead, felled by the bullets of your conquering
Soldiers! Yet you would not let a little child live!
How can you claim to be strong, when your minds
Are so feeble? O child, how shall I mourn you?
Insane animals, the Ijebus and the Ifes have crushed your brain,
Made a mess of those lovely tresses that your mother
Spent several fond moments braiding! You could have grown
Into a splendid man. You could have been successful and happy,
At least as happy as the gods permit us in this world.
You could have inherited your father's estates,

59

Prolonged his renown. But, my child, all that you have
To inherit now is this garment, which I wrap about you.
Ah life is a joke, my friends. Let no one count herself lucky
Till she finds herself on her death bed.
Come forward now, one by one, and pay your homage.
A little sand on his eyelids is all we can manage,
And your songs to see him home.
(The dirge, 'Şe mba mọ' rises, as the women file around the body.)

CHORUS: Child, please forgive us for bringing you to the world
And having to send you away so early and so harshly

WOMAN: You have fallen, not for your skill in the field of war like your fathers

WOMAN: Gone, not for standing tall on the trunk of some memorable ideal

WOMAN: You have gone, son, because of the errors of a wanton woman!

WOMAN: Boys of your age should be learning how to say your first words

WOMAN: Learning the riddles the Owu alone speak to the wind to tame it

WOMAN: Boys of your age should be growing muscles for handling a spear

WOMAN: A chest to dare danger, and a heart to hold the tender moments

WOMAN: But here you are already a corpse, far from your initiation night!

WOMAN: Tears! See how our tears are falling...

WOMAN: Forgive us for not covering you in magnificent robes as you deserve

WOMAN: Forgive us for not decorating you in the coral beads of kingship

WOMAN: Forgive us, child, for dressing you only with sand and our tears
(Some women carry the body away for burial, as ERELU screams.)

60

CHORUS LEADER: Erelu, take heart. If you break now,
What shall we do?

ERELU: The gods are not worth much! They lie and lie all the time
And deceive us! They will take all our sacrifices,
Wear us down in supplication, but they have their own designs
On us all the time! Did we not pray enough? Did we not offer
Sacrifice upon sacrifice! Yet see what they have made
Of our city! The gods are not worth much respect!

CHORUS: Careful, Erelu! We beg you, restrain yourself. A word
Against the gods, and even worse things may still come upon us!

WOMAN: It's already happening: see! The palace is on fire again!
*(General exclamations. Enter GESINDE with a detail of
soldiers.)*

GESINDE: We're clearing out, so the orders were to burn everything
That still remains standing. Women, soon you'll hear
The horns. That will be the signal for all of us.
You will file down immediately, in an orderly fashion,
And join the caravan. If I may inform you, beauty
Has conquered once again, as before. That celebrated slut
Has regained Mayé's heart, and joined his caravan. Yes,
Iyunloye is riding back with us in triumph!
(The women exclaim.)
No, don't sigh, don't even bother. It is the logic of victory,
The logic of defeat. Such is the justice of the great.
(To ERELU). As for you, Erelu, please follow these soldiers.
They will take you to Balogun Derin.

ERELU: My women, it is time to say goodbye.

CHORUS LEADER: No, Erelu, not yet! In spite of your bitterness,
I beg you, remember who you are, what you still have to do.

61

GESINDE: What does she mean?

CHORUS LEADER: Erelu understands. She is the mother of the city, the only
Mouth we have left now to speak to our ancestors.

ERELU: No, no, let me go...

CHORUS LEADER: I know how you feel, Erelu, but Kabiyesi,
Your husband, is no longer here. All our priests and
Princes have been turned to corpses. Their bodies lie around
In the rubble there, unburied. They and the other victims
Need someone to release their spirits and send them back
Safely home to the ancestors, someone trained in the task.
Among us there's no such person left now,
Except you.

ERELU: My friends, you don't understand. This is no longer
The Erelu you knew, but just another corpse still talking.
Grief has drained out my powers. Besides,
As you can see, these soldiers are in a hurry—

CHORUS LEADER: They'll wait, I'm sure, if we ask them. Or
Won't you, Gesinde? Just a few seconds.

GESINDE: A few seconds for what?

CHORUS LEADER: It's not for the ears of strangers. But Erelu knows
What we must do to save our future from eternal damnation. It is
A duty she cannot evade or refuse. We won't be long.

GESINDE: I'm afraid, I can not—

CHORUS LEADER: You are from Ife, soldier! A bush place, we know, but
Will you say that even there, the living owe no obligations to the dead?

62

ERELU: Please leave us for a while, Gesinde, you and your soldiers.
She's right. It is a duty only a few among us are raised to perform
At such moments. Go now, we will catch up with you.

GESINDE: Well then, we'll go. You know I am not unkind.
But let it be very brief. The generals, as I told you,
Are in a hurry, and it won't be pleasant at all
If I have to send my men back to fetch you.
(He leaves, with the soldiers.)

CHORUS LEADER: Thank you, Erelu. Now our dead will not be left
To wander forever like abandoned mongrels
In the wastelands of the after-life...

ERELU: No, don't thank me! I'll do my duty, since
You insist. But
Even the ancestors know it's only my carrion
Left now to sing to them.

CHORUS LEADER: Then perhaps you should not do it. It is dangerous,
As you know, to seek to meet the dead, unless you are strong
In both body and spirit—

ERELU: Let us proceed. It shall not be said, while I live,
That Erelu saw the post holding up the land's ceiling tottering
And shrank away like a coward. My dear women,
Begin, you know the songs:
Join these old bones in our ritual valediction to the dead.
*(The Women begin the dirge, 'Àtùpà gbépo nlç félépo',
till they gradually separate into two Choruses dancing
around the figure of ERELU. The dances are slow and
ritually ceremonial, and will gradually conduct ERELU
and the Chorus Leaders into a trance.)*

63

ERELU: Let this be our dance of defeat, our final dirge
To our wrecked city, to perfidy, the folly of war.
Dance with me now the dance of our death!

CHORUS LEADER 1: We dance—
For those who fell in the field of slaughter

CHORUS LEADER 2: We dance—
For all who fell to feed the greed of power

CHORUS LEADER 1: We dance—
For all the innocent silenced in their prime,
Silenced so that someone could win an argument

CHORUS LEADER 2: We dance—
For the numerous souls wasted again and again
In the ceaseless clash of liberty and lust

CHORUS LEADER 1: We dance—
For the widows and orphans who survive
But who will soon be drawn into fresh confrontations

CHORUS LEADER 2: We dance—
For the numerous ghosts we leave behind
For the bodies abandoned on these broken bricks

CHORUS LEADER 1: For them, we summon you, Anlugbua! Come!

CHORUS LEADER 2: Come, Anlugbua! Come down!

CHORUS LEADER 1: Come, Anlugbua, come down! Máa bò, Anlugbua, sò kalè!

CHORUS LEADER 2: Máa bò, Anlugbua, sò kalè!

WOMEN: Máa bò, Anlugbua, sò kalè!
(This call is taken up now by the two Choruses, till it swells

64

into an incantatory chant. At the climax of it, ERELU dances forward, possessed, and has to be restrained by many hands. At the same moment, caught in a spotlight, the god ANLUGBUA himself appears and stands watching the scene.)

CHORUS LEADER 1: Is it you, ancestral father? Is it you?

ERELU: *(Her voice changed now, in the god's possession).*
Yes, I have come, I, Anlugbua. Why do you call me?

CHORUS LEADER 2: Home is where every traveller returns after a journey,
However long. When night falls, the visitor must take his leave
Of his hosts. But this strange night came suddenly upon us
In the market of the world, even before we could gather our lamps.

ERELU: I hear you...

CHORUS LEADER 1: Our people must go home, father. No swimmer, however good,
Can swim beyond the rim of the world. This world's journey
Has ended in catastrophe for us. Without your help,
We can no longer find our way back in the void.

ERELU: I cannot help you—

CHORUS LEADER 2: What, ancestral father?

ERELU: You were given this life. You chose to waste it
In a senseless quarrel over a woman—

ERELU: It was not our fault, you must know.
The generals gave the orders, we only obeyed.

CHORUS LEADER 1: And now, you have to pay—

65

CHORUS LEADER 2: Please, help us! You are our father, you cannot desert us—

ERELU: A father can only chew for a child; he cannot swallow for her.
If only you had read your history right, the lessons
Left behind by the ancestors! Each of us, how else did we go
Except by the wrath of war? Each of us,
Demolished through violence and contention! Not so?
But you chose to glorify the story with lies! Lies!
Our apotheosis as you sing it is a fraud!

CHORUS LEADER 2: We did not know, we common folk! Forgive us,
It is the rulers who write history—

CHORUS LEADER 1: It is the hunters who compose the story of the hunt—

CHORUS LEADER 2: It is the revellers, not the slaughtered cows,
Who record the fable of the feast!

ERELU: Then the deer must train themselves to seize the gun from
Their hunters! The cows to take over the narration of
Their own story. Perhaps
After the punishment that's coming for you—

BOTH CHORUS LEADER: Punishment! Have mercy, ancestor!

ERELU: I cannot help you. No one can. You are going now into years
Of wandering and slavery. As the penalty for your wasted lives.
Perhaps afterwards you would have learnt the wisdom
Of sticking together, and loving one another...

WOMEN: Father!

ERELU: No, enough! I must go now. Goodbye!...

WOMEN: Mercy! We beg for—

66

(ERELU utters a long scream and collapses. It takes a while before they realise that she is dead. They rush towards her in consternation, and then freeze, singing 'Wẹlẹ-wẹlẹ leri nsẹ o...' ANLUGBUA begins to speak into the silence.)

ANLUGBUA: Poor human beings! War is what will destroy you!
As it destroys the gods. But I am moved, and I promise:
Owu will rise again! Not here,
Not as a single city again—Mother will not permit that,
I know—but in little communities elsewhere,
Within other cities of Yorubaland. Those now going
Into slavery shall start new kingdoms in those places.
It's the only atonement a god can make for you
Against your ceaseless volition for self-destruction.
You human beings, always thirsty for blood,
Always eager to devour one another! I hope
History will teach you. I hope you will learn. Farewell.
(The Women's dirge begins to rise now.)

BLACKOUT. END OF PLAY

Appendix: Songs and Dirges Used

Note: The songs in the play consist largely of dirges, bride chants (*ekún ìyàwó*) and *oríkì* (praise poems) and are heavily based on the corresponding generic structures of traditional Yòrùbá music. This means that their essence is to be distilled more from the mood and atmosphere they create - through the songs' rhythmic patterns and metaphorical richness, the chanters' voice manipulation, emotional involvement and evocative power, as well as the audience's willingness to collaborate - than from the actual, literal meaning of the lines. Like all music, therefore, their full effect cannot be fully grasped from a mere understanding of the words.

The following 'translation' is therefore merely a guide, and will help the musician who understands Yòrùbá, but probably not all its dialectal inflections. It is better to just listen to the songs till they translate themselves to the inner ear, and then sing them like that, in affective response.

(-FO)

YORUBA ENGLISH TRANSLATION

(1) **Àtùpà gbépo nlẹ fẹlẹpo** (Lamp, yield your oil to the oil seller)

Àtùpà gbépo nlẹ fẹlẹpo:

Lamp, yield your oil to the oil seller

—*Refrain* :
Ìràwọ wọ, ọrùn ò ràn,
Oṣùpá ò tàn mọ ò,
alẹ lẹ lẹ?

—*Refrain* :
The stars are down, the sun retired,
The moon's refused to light
the night

Àlejò ló dé lọ́gànjọ́ òru
—*Refrain* : Ìràwọ wọ, *etc...*
Alágàngan ló k"ọ́jà rẹ dé o
—*Refrain* : Ìràwọ wọ, *etc...*
Ọjà oró rẹ ló mà ko dé o :
—*Refrain* : Ìràwọ wọ, *etc...*
Oró ikú dẹ ni tAlágàngan!
—*Refrain* : Ìràwọ wọ, *etc...*
Kò mà sẹni tó le yèé bọ o !
—*Refrain* : Ìràwọ wọ, *etc...*
Àtùpà gbépo nlẹ fẹlẹpo :
—*Refrain* : Ìràwọ wọ *etc...*

A stranger's come in the dead of night
The stars are down, etc...
Alágàngan* has come with his wares
The stars are down, etc...
Has brought his merchandise of pain
The stars are down, etc...
Death of course is what he sells
The stars are down, etc...
And none of us can refuse to buy
The stars are down, etc...
Lamp, yield your oil to the oil seller
The stars are down, etc...

(2) **Lèsí ma gbàwá ò**

(Who will save us?)

Lèsí ma gbàwá ò
—*Refrain* : Tere jìna !
Lèsí kà rè dìmú ?
—*Refrain* : Tere jìna !

Who will save us ?
—*Refrain* : Tere jina!
'Who shall we hang on to?
—*Refrain* : Tere jina!

---

* This is another name for Death

Afárá já lÓwú!   Owu's bridge has collapsed!
—*Refrain* : Tere jìna!   —*Refrain* : Tere jina!
Ogun iná ti gbòde !   The war of fire has broken out!
—*Refrain* : Tere jìna !   —*Refrain* : Tere jìna!
Yéèpà, ọkọ mi !   What a calamity, my husband!
—*Refrain* : Tere jìna !   —*Refrain* : Tere jina!
Yéèpà, aya mi!   What a disaster, my wife!
—*Refrain* : Tere jìna !   —*Refrain* : Tere jìna!
Mò? yàgò, ọmọ mi!   Run away, my child!
—*Refrain* : Tere jìna !   —*Refrain* : Tere jina!
Ogun iná ti gbòde !   The war fire is everywhere !
—*Refrain* : Tere jìna !   —*Refrain* : Tere jìna!

(3) *Lèsí gbọ́ gbìgbì léreko o?* (Who heard the frightening sound on
the farm?)

Lèsí gbọ́ gbìgbì léreko o?   Who heard the frightening sound on
— — gbìgbì!   the farm? — gbìgbì!
Bóo gbọ́ gbìgbì ko wá sọ o   If you did, come and say o —
— gbìgbì!   gbìgbì!
Wọ́n wípé igi nlá wó — ẹhn!??   They say a big tree's fallen — ẹhn!??
Èmi gbọ́ gbìgbì léreko o gbìgbì!   I didn't hear the sound at all - gbìgbì!
Èmi gbọ́ gbìgbì léreko o —   I certainly did not hear the sound!
gbìgbì   gbìgbì!
Lèsí gbọ́ gbìgbì lágbàlá ó?   Who heard the scream in — the yard?
gbìgbì! —   gbìgbì!
Bóo gbọ́ gbìgbì ko wá sọ o --   If you did, come and say so —
gbìgbì ! —   gbìgbì —
Wọ́n wípé ẹni nlá ṣubú —   They say a giant has fallen —
ẹhn!??   ẹhn!??
Èmi gbọ́ gbìgbì lágbàlá o —   I heard no scream in the yard—
gbìgbì!   gbìgbì!

Èmi gbọ́ gbìgbì lágbàlá o — gbìgbì!	I heard no scream in the yard! — gbìgbì!
Lèsí gbọ́ gbìgbì lọ́dẹ̀dẹ̀ o? — gbìgbì!	Who heard the scream on the balcony? — gbìgbì!
Bóo gbọ́ gbìgbì ko wá sọ o — gbìgbì!	If you did, come and say so — gbìgbì!
Èmi gbọ́ gbìgbì lọ́dẹ̀dẹ̀ o — gbìgbì!	I heard no cry on the balcony — gbìgbì!
Wọ́n wípé ẹyin nla fọ́ – ẹhn!??	They say a big egg has cracked – ẹhn!??
Èmi gbọ́ gbìgbì lọ́dẹ̀dẹ̀ o – . gbìgbì!	I heard no cry on the balcony — gbìgbì!
Èmi gbọ́ gbìgbì lọ́dẹ̀dẹ̀ o – — gbìgbì!	I heard no cry on the balcony — — gbìgbì
Lèsí gbọ́ gbìgbì lojúde o? — gbìgbì!	Who heard the scream on the — gbìgbì! doorstep?
Bóo gbọ́ gbìgbì ko wá sọ o — gbìgbì!	If you did, come and say so — gbìgbì!
Wọ́n wípé baálé ṣubú — ẹhn!??	They say the family head fainted — ẹhn!
Èmi gbọ́ gbìgbì lojúde o — gbìgbì!	I heard no cry on the doorstep – gbìgbì!
Èmi gbọ́ gbìgbì lojúde o — gbìgbì!	I heard no scream at all! — gbìgbì!

(4) Ìjì ayé pọ̀ (The storms of life are many)

Ìjì ayé pọ̀ ?	The storms of life are many
Ogun gbòde o	War has broken out
A ti ṣe títí	If we've tried all we could
Tí ò já sí nkankan:	And yet to no avail
Ayé á sú ni,	We'll be frustrated
Kálára gbé nkan jẹ !	To the point of suicide! (by poisoning)

71

Ìyá ṣagídí,	Mother braved all
Ìyá mà kú o	But Mother died
Bàbá ṣagbára,	Father tried his best
Tí ò já sí nkankan:	All to no avail
Gbogbo ilé ti tú	The family's scattered
Kálàṛẹ mókùn so !	To drive one to suicide (by hanging)
Níbo lá wá nlọ ?	Where are we going
Ile ẹrú ni:	But to the house of slavery?
A sunkún títí	We've cried our eyes dry
Tí ò já sí nkankan :	All to no avail
Ayé ti sú ni,	We're tired of life
Kálára gbé nkan mu!...	To the point of suicide (by poisoning)

(5) Ẹ súre fún mi (Shower me with blessings)

Ẹ súre fún mi	Shower me with blessings
Mò nrelé ọkọ	I am going to my husband's house
Ẹ sì bá mi yọ̀	And rejoice with me
Mò nrelé ọkọ	As I head for my matrimonial book
Òkùnkùn paradà	Darkness, melt away
Ìmọ́lẹ̀ tẹlé mi lọ	And light, accompany me
Ẹ bá mi yọ̀ ṣẹ̀ṣẹ̀	Come, celebrate with me
Sẹ̀sẹ̀ la nyọ̀ mọkọ	A groom is met with rejoicing

(6) Ọlọ́bẹ̀ ló lọkọ o (Husbands are won by those who can cook)

Ọlọ́bẹ̀ ló lọkọ o	Husbands are for those who can cook
— Èmi ti rọkọ fẹ́ o-e!	— See, I've won my own husband!
Ọkọ mà wọ́n lóde o :	Husbands are hard to find:
— Èmi ti rí tèmi o e !	— But I've got my own husband !
Ọkùnrin wọ́n lóde o :	Good men are rare to find
— Èmi ti rí tèmi o e !	— But I caught my own !

Ogun tí gbé wọn tán o	Wars have made them rare to find:
— Èmi ti rí tèmi o e!	– But I've found my own !
Baba ó dìgbà ná	Father, goodbye to you :
— Èmi nlọ lé ọkọ o e !	—As I leave for my husband's home!
Ìyá ẹ má sunkún o	Mother, wipe your tears :
— Èmi nlọlé ọkọ·o e ! !	—I'm going to my husband's house !

(7) Jọ̀wọ́ o dúró,sisí (Please, baby, give me a second)

Jọ̀wọ́ o dúró,sisí	Please, baby, give me a second
Sisí lóun ò dúró:	But I won't wait, she says
Gbà mí lọ́rọ̀ kan	Can I have a word with you?
Sisí lóun ò mà ṣe	She says she's not interested
Sisí lóun ò dúró:	And won't wait, she says
Kíló nkán ẹ lójú	But why in such a hurry?
Sisí ò, kí ló dé?	Baby, what's the matter?.
Ọrọ̀ ọkọ ni	It's a husband matter
Ṣùgbọ́n kò lè yé ẹ !	But you cannot understand
Kò lè yé ẹ rárá.!	You can't understand at all
Òrìṣáyè nlọ	Orisaye is leaving
Ọkọ mò nbá lọ !...	Leaving with my husband!..:

(8) Wẹlẹ-wẹlẹ lèrì nsẹ́ o   (Softly, softly falls the dew)

Wẹlẹ-wẹlẹ lèrì nsẹ́ o	Softly, softly falls the dew
Wẹlẹ-wẹlẹ lèrì o	Softly, softly the dew
Ṣẹ́wẹlẹ ṣẹwẹlẹ lòjò alẹ́lẹ́ o	Gently, gently rain in the evening
Ṣẹwẹlẹ ṣẹwẹlẹ lòjò	Gently falls the evening rain
Ikú ò ní gbowó	Death will not accept money ·
Ikú ò ní gbẹ̀bẹ̀?	Death will not listen to any plea
A kígbe-kígbe oró Ikú	Repeatedly we curse death's sting
Ikú ò lóògùn o ! ·	But there's no medicine for Death!

73

(9) Ọ̀run dẹ̀dẹ̀ẹ̀dẹ̀ bí orin arò (The hereafter, like a dirge)

(Solo / Repeat)

(a)

Ọ̀run dẹ̀dẹ̀ẹ̀dẹ̀ bí orin arò
Òyígíyigì, a ti rúbọ
A ò yí padà, a ó darúgbó
Òyígíyigì, Ọba omi
Títííti lorí ogbó
Òyígíyigì, Ọba omi
A ti rúbọ ìyè, Olúyẹ́yẹ́ntuyẹ́?
·A ti rúbọ àgbà, Olúyẹ́yẹ́ntuyẹ́?
Àkàlàmàgbò kìí kú léwe!

(a)

The hereafter, like a dirge
Mighty Father, we have sacrificed
Let's not die, till we reach old age
Mighty Father, God of waters
Long, long lasts the head of grey
Mighty Father, God of waters
We bid for long life, for grey hair
We bid to grow old, Father of elders
Just as the vulture never dies young

(b)

Kìí kú lèwe! Éìkú léwe!
— Àkàlàmàgbò kìí kú léwe !
Títííti lorí ogbó
— Àkàlàmàgbò kìí kú léwe!
Àní bá pejò lejò opa
— Àkàlàmàgbò kìí kú léwe !
Àní bá pejò lejò opa
— Àkàlàmàgbò kìí kú léwe !
Ọ̀rúnmìlà á ṣẹ́ wọn nítan
Ṣẹ́ wọn nítan
Ṣẹ́ wọn nítan
Ṣẹ́ wọn nítan

(b)

Never dies young, never dies young!
— The vulture never dies young
Long, long lasts the head of grey
— The vulture never dies young!
Who insults us will not grow old
— The vulture never dies young!
Who summons Snake will die by him
— The vulture never dies young
Diviner god will break their legs !
Break their legs
Break their legs
Break their legs…

(The line is repeated over and over again now, hysterically, as the women become possessed)

(10) *Bùjé-bùjé pa mí o*   (I've been stung to death)

Bùjé-bùjé pa mí o : *Tere bùjé!*   I've been stung to death : *Tere bùjé!*
Òyin nlá tá mí o: *Tere bùjé!*   Stung by a mighty bee : *Tere bùjé!*
Ikú gbé mi lọmọ lọ: *Tere bùjé!*   Death's stolen my child: *Tere bùjé!*
Ikú dá mi lóró : *Tere bùjé!*   Death's stung me badly : *Tere bùjé!*
Bùjé-bùjé pa mí o !....   I've been stung to death : *Tere bùjé!*

(11) *Adeoti's oriki :Ọmọọ́ mi Adéòtí* (My child Adeoti)

Ọmọọ́ mi Adéòtí	My child Adeoti
Ọmọ Ánlugbùà	Descendant of Anlugbua
Ánlugbùà	Ánlugbùà
Ògún forí olú ṣeré	'Ogun that played with a crown
Ọmọ Asunkúngbadé	And won a crown with tears,
Ọmọ Àgbàoyè	Son of Àgbaoye'
Ọmọ Àrèmabọ̀ Ágbádéṣíré,	Offspring of Aremabo Agbadesire
Ọmọ	Daughter of
'Láì gbé iyùn sọ́rùn,	'Even without royal neck beads
Dídán ní ndán bíi idẹ!'	She gleams and gleams like brass! »
Ah Ọmọ mi Ọpẹ́nlẹ́ngẹ́,	Ah, my slim and pretty daughter,
Ọrun re o	Rest in peace
Bóò bá dọrun,	O there in heaven, don't eat worms
Má jekòló	Don't eat millipedes
Oun wọn bá njẹ ni o bá wọn jẹ...	Eat only what they eat there...

(12) *Ṣé mbá mọ̀, mi ò ni wálé ayé* (If I'd known, I'd not have come
                                         to the world)

Ṣé mbá mọ̀, mi ò ni wálé ayé   If I'd known, I'd not have come to
                                            the world

Mbá sinmi o, sájùlé òrun	I'd have stayed peacefully in heaven instead

— *Refrain:*

Rògbòdìyòn ayé yi tí pò jù	*Too many tribulations fill the world*
Ìpónjú ojó, ìpónjú òru,	Hardship all day long, hardship at night,
Ìpónjú òórò Ìpónjú òsán,	Hardship in the morning and afternoon,
Sé mbá mò, mbá sinmi	*If I'd known, I'd have stayed back*
ní tèmi	*in heaven*

Obìnrin bímo tán, ó mí sunkún	A woman gives birth and begins to cry
Abiyamo njó, ogún gbòde	As nursing mothers rejoice, war breaks out
Èjìrè ìsokùn ló mà tún sòfò	The (mother of) twins will soon be mourning

— *Refrain:*

Okùnrin ògbòogbòjo, ó debo Ògún	The handsome turn sacrifice to the god of war
Akín rogun, kò mà dèhìnbò	The brave go to battle and never return
Kí là mbímo fún bí ó ní dàgbà?	Why have children then, if they won't last?

— *Refrain:*

(13) *Dóko dóko o* : (Unfaithful woman!)

Dóko dóko o :	Unfaithful woman!
— *Refrain* : Panságà!	—*Refrain* : *Adulteress !*
E wojú òdóko !	Behold her face!
— *Refrain* : Panságà !	—*Refrain* : *Adulteress !*
Àgbèrè obìnrin !	Fornicator!
— *Refrain* : Panságà !	—*Refrain* : *Adulteress !*
Àgbèrè obìnrin !	Second-hand woman!
— *Refrain* : Panságà !	—*Refrain* : *Adulteress !*
Yatan è, kí nwolé !	Open wide her legs for me !

— *Refrain* : Panṣágà !
Ṣíi sílẹ̀, kí nrokà !
— *Refrain* : Panṣágà !
Dọ́kọ dọ́kọ o :
— *Refrain* : Panṣágà !
Àgbèrè obìnrin!
— *Refrain* : Panṣágà !

—*Refrain* : *Adulteress* !
Open and let me stroke hard !
—*Refrain* : *Adulteress* !
Unfaithful woman!
—*Refrain* : *Adulteress* !
Shameless slut!
—*Refrain* : *Adulteress* !

(14) Òjò ayọ̀ kán sí mi lára (Showers of joy fell on me)

Ee! Ee !	Ee! Ee!
Òjò ayọ̀ kán sí mi lára	Showers of joy fell on me
Ẹ ní nní jó !	And you say I shouldn't dance ?
Ẹ̀rì ìdúnnún sẹ́ sí mi lára	The dew of joy fell on me
Lóòréré !	From afar off !
Bẹ̀rẹ̀ o... bẹ̀rẹ̀ !	Bend, oh bend !
Ọ̀rẹ́ mi ṣóo gbọ́ ?	My friend, are you listening ?
Bẹ̀rẹ̀ o... bẹ̀rẹ̀ !	Bend, oh bend!
Ijó ni kóo jó :	And dance to it !
Orin... orin.....	Sing, oh sing !
Orin lẹ́nu rẹ̀ !	Fill your mouth with song!

(15) Aderogun's oriki.: Ọmọ mi Àdérógun (My son, Aderogun !)

Ọmọ mi Adérógun,	My son, Aderogun !
Ò wá di bàbáá mi lóni!	You become my father today !
Tó bá délé kó bá mi kíwon:	When you get home, give them my greetings :
Adérógun, Òkìkí olú	Aderogun, brave one
Ó digbéré,ọ́ dàrìnnàkò !	Farewell, till we meet again !
Ọmọ Jagunmólú	Son of the warrior Jagunmolu
Ọmọ Ará Òwu òjògèdèngbé!	Offspring of Owu's ancestors

Ọmọ "Jagun májolè,	Son of « Fight, don't steal,
Mira-milè má milé ẹbí,	Shake men, shake the earth, but not your in-laws,
Ẹbí ẹni ni ngbé ni gá !	For in-laws dignify us !'
Ọmọ « Wọn gbé mi sọnlè lÁpòmù	Son of « 'I was felled (fighting) in 'Apomu
Ìyẹn ìí ṣọmọọ mi ! »	Cannot be my child »
Ò korí-korí ò korí ọmọ tuntun :	Collector of heads except the newborn's
Wàá sùn, wàá jí,	Sleep on, but you will rise again
Oò ní jọkùn, oò ní jekòló :	You'll not eat millipedes or worms:
Tó bá délé kó bá mi kíwọn	When you get home there, say my greetings :
Kóo pé mò mbọ̀ lọ́nà o......	And tell them I am on my way!'

(16) **Ara mi, ẹ woro tiku fi ṣe wa,** (Come see the pain they put on us)

Ara mi, ẹ woro tiku fi ṣe wa,	Come, see the pain they put on us
Paga, ẹ woya ta waye wa ba!	That we came to meet on earth

Ẹyin le pe ka lọkọ lo tọ	You taught us it's right to wed,
Ẹyin le pe kọlọkọ loyun	Right too to become pregnant
Ẹyin lẹ pe koloyun ko sọ?	And afterwards give birth
Koloyun sọ, ka bimọ saye	And have children on earth

Ṣẹyin lẹ tun lọ sile Iku	Was it you also went to Death
Ṣẹyin le peku ko da wa loro	And brought him here to strike us?
Ẹyin le da"na ogun saye	Was it you also lit the fire of war
Ẹ fọmọ ṣofo, sọ wọn di eeru	And burnt our young to ashes?

78

Lightning Source UK Ltd.
Milton Keynes UK
UKHW04f0610170818
327343UK00001B/57/P

9 789780 690267